Werner Herzog

PHILOSOPHICAL FILMMAKERS

Series editor: Costica Bradatan is a Professor of Humanities at Texas Tech University, USA, and an Honorary Research Professor of Philosophy at the University of Queensland, Australia. He is the author of *Dying for Ideas: The Dangerous Lives of the Philosophers* (Bloomsbury, 2015), among other books.

Films can ask big questions about human existence: what it means to be alive, to be afraid, to be moral, to be loved. The *Philosophical Filmmakers* series examines the work of influential directors, through the writing of thinkers wanting to grapple with the rocky territory where film and philosophy touch borders.

Each book involves a philosopher engaging with an individual filmmaker's work, revealing how it has inspired the author's own philosophical perspectives and how critical engagement with those films can expand our intellectual horizons.

Other titles in the series:
Erich Rohmer, Vittorio Hösle

Other titles forthcoming:
Alfred Hitchcock, Mark Roche
Jacques Tati, John Ó Maoilearca
Shyam Benegal, Samir Chopra
Terrence Malick, Robert Sinnerbrink

Werner Herzog

Filmmaker and Philosopher

Richard Eldridge,
Swarthmore College, USA

BLOOMSBURY ACADEMIC
LONDON • NEW YORK • OXFORD • NEW DELHI • SYDNEY

BLOOMSBURY ACADEMIC
Bloomsbury Publishing Plc
50 Bedford Square, London, WC1B 3DP, UK
1385 Broadway, New York, NY 10018, USA

BLOOMSBURY, BLOOMSBURY ACADEMIC and the Diana logo
are trademarks of Bloomsbury Publishing Plc

First published in Great Britain 2019
Reprinted 2019

Cover design: Irene Martinez-Costa
Cover image: Courtesy Everett Collection / Mary Evans

Bloomsbury Publishing Plc does not have any control over, or responsibility
for, any third-party websites referred to or in this book. All internet addresses
given in this book were correct at the time of going to press. The author and
publisher regret any inconvenience caused if addresses have changed or sites
have ceased to exist, but can accept no responsibility for any such changes.

A catalogue record for this book is available from the British Library.

A catalog record for this book is available from the Library of Congress.

ISBN: HB: 978-1-3500-9167-2
       PB: 978-1-3501-0015-2
       ePDF: 978-1-3500-9166-5
       eBook: 978-1-3500-9168-9

Series: Philosophical Filmmakers

Typeset by Integra Software Services Pvt. Ltd.
Printed and bound in Great Britain

To find out more about our authors and books visit www.bloomsbury.com
and sign up for our newsletters.

In memory of Stanley Bates

But generally, it is not understood yet that a problem of the same magnitude is that we do not have adequate images, and that's what I'm working on—a new grammar of images.

—WERNER HERZOG, IN *WERNER HERZOG EATS HIS SHOE*
(DIR. LES BLANK, 1980)

Essence is expressed by grammar.

—LUDWIG WITTGENSTEIN, *PHILOSOPHICAL INVESTIGATIONS*, §371

To submit to this displacement [that occurs in the work of art] means: to transform our accustomed ties to world and to earth and henceforth to restrain all usual doing and prizing, knowing and looking, in order to stay within the truth that is happening in the work.

—MARTIN HEIDEIGGER, "THE ORIGIN OF THE WORK OF ART"

Contents

List of Figures

Acknowledgments

It is a pleasure to be able to express my thanks in writing at the head of this book to the friends who have been companions in its simmering, forty-year gestation, as I have been watching, thinking about, and talking with others about Herzog's films. During the late 1970s in Chicago, Paul Gudel, Ruth Melville, Stephen Melville, Joan Vandegrift, and I eagerly awaited and then often saw the newest Herzog release together, and my sense of what is going on in the films was shaped at the very beginning by our conversations about them. The American Society for Aesthetics has been a home for my thinking about the arts and film in particular throughout my professional life, and I am especially indebted to and grateful for the continuing presence there of Stanley Bates, also my teacher. The character of my interest in aesthetics and film is inconceivable without his sharp perceptiveness, wide learning, and generous encouragements. Thomas Wartenberg has also been a regular ASA presence and friend in my thinking about film. Over the past ten or so years, my life and my work in aesthetics have been greatly enriched by the Philadelphia area Aesthetics Reading Group, ably, graciously, and generously hosted by Susan Feagin, and including most often Sally Banes, Noël Carroll, John Carvalho, Robert Clewis, Kristin Gjesdal, Paul Guyer, Espen Hammer, and Mary Wiseman, as well as occasional visitors. We read together and discussed a number of recent studies in the aesthetics of film, as in the philosophy of art generally. Inevitably I learned something from these discussions, and what I learned has figured steadily in this book.

I am grateful to my students in my classes in the philosophy of film at Swarthmore College, to whom I have shown *Aguirre* and with whom I have discussed general film aesthetics. Their responses to both the films and the theory have been continuous encouragements to me. The writing of this book was generously supported by a Mary Albertson Faculty Fellowship from Swarthmore College that enabled its timely completion. Costica Bradatan conceived the series in which this book appears, invited my contribution to it, and encouraged me throughout the period of writing; the book would not exist otherwise.

Anyone working on Werner Herzog is indebted not only to the films themselves but also to the massive, indispensable, and entrancing *Werner Herzog—A Guide for the Perplexed: Conversations with Paul Cronin* (London: Faber and Faber, 2014), cited in the body of the text below simply as Cronin. Herzog's written thoughts about his life and work, elicited by Cronin's deeply informed and indefatigable questioning, and carefully reconsidered and extended by Herzog from the first, 2002, edition of the book (*Herzog on Herzog* [London: Faber and Faber, 2002]) to the 2014 edition are themselves a work of significant literary and philosophical value, and they have guided me throughout my own thinking about the films. Coupled with his writings, Herzog's films support my conviction—part of the argument of this book—that they engage originally and compellingly, by way of images, with issues about meaning and value in a way that contributes to and compares well with the most important contemporary philosophy. They have helped me to think better than I would have otherwise.

During the summer of 2017, I began systematically re-watching many Herzog films and watching some that I had not known previously. Two philosophers—Rafael Azize and Jay Miller—watched a number of these films with me and talked with me afterward not only about them, but also about film and philosophy, contemporary philosophy, and contemporary culture more broadly. The pleasures of their company and the cogency of their insights have improved this book.

Joan Vandegrift read every word of the manuscript as it came into existence and improved many of them, as well as watching and talking about nearly every Herzog film with me. These are labors of love on her part that ought not to be taken for granted, so I won't, but will instead thank her for them, as for everything else.

1

Introduction: Images and Contemporary Culture

Think about the dancing chicken in Stroszek, *which people never forget, even if they have no memory of anything else in the film.*
—WERNER HERZOG (CRONIN, 236)

I first saw a number of Werner Herzog films during the late 1970s in Chicago—*Aguirre, the Wrath of God* (1972), *The Enigma of Kaspar Hauser* (1974), *Heart of Glass* (1976), *Stroszek* (1976), and *Nosferatu* (1979)—at showings at Facets Multimedia, the Art Institute of Chicago, and Doc Films at the University of Chicago. My attention was called to these films by the rich Chicago film review culture, including Gene Siskel at the *Chicago Tribune*, Dave Kehr at the *Chicago Reader*, and, especially, Roger Ebert, Herzog's friend and interlocutor at the *Chicago Sun Times*. I remember in particular the sustained shot of the rapids of the Rio Urubamba near the beginning of *Aguirre* as wondrously and mysteriously transfixing, affording a sense of nature as suffused with a self-developing power that surrounded human life, eluded definite comprehension, and yet was somehow captured by the camera's extended perfect attention. This affordance of obscure sense was repeated in the shots of the fog flowing through mountain passes in *Heart of Glass* and *Nosferatu*, as well as by the extraordinary shot in *Stroszek* of the repossessed trailer being towed to the right out of the frame, leaving only the vast Wisconsin prairie emptily filling the entire field of view of both *Stroszek* and the viewer. In each case, I immediately knew these shots and the films that housed them were something extraordinary—paradigm instances of the powers of art— and I have now been thinking about these filmic achievements—as well as viewing further films and teaching some of these central ones, especially *Aguirre*—for some forty years.

As a result of these initial experiences and continuing history, as well as of the fact that I am a working philosopher, this book is substantially different from much contemporary academic film theory. Herzog has himself criticized academic film study sharply:

> Academia stifles cinema, encircling it like a liana vine wraps round a tree, smothering and draining away all life. Construct films, don't deconstruct them. Create poetry, don't destroy it. Whenever I encounter film theorists, I lower my head and charge. ... You would learn more about filmmaking during [a long] journey [on foot] than if you spent five years at film school. Your experiences would be the very opposite of academic knowledge, for academia is the death of cinema. Somebody who has been a boxer in Africa would be better trained as a filmmaker than if he had graduated from one of the "best" film schools in the world. All that counts is real life. (Cronin, 178, 213)

This sharply critical stance on Herzog's part extends in particular to academic studies of his own films:

> On the table in front of us is a pile of academic articles about my films that you brought over for me to look at. The minute you leave

here today, it will all be thrown into the trash. The healthiest thing anyone can do is avoid that impenetrable nonsense. My response to it all is a blank stare, just as I respond to most philosophical writings. I can't crack the code of Hegel and Heidegger; it isn't the concepts that are alien to me, but I get my ideas from real life, not books. When I hear the kind of language used by zealots and film theorists, Venetian blinds start rattling down. (Cronin, 177)

Although I have read and learned from both film theory in general and Herzog film scholarship in particular, I also significantly share Herzog's worries about these bodies of work. But note two things about Herzog's critical remarks: (1) they imply some acquaintance with Hegel, Heidegger, and philosophy more broadly (acquaintance that most contemporary film scholars lack) and (2) Herzog emphasizes the importance of poetry and literature, for him and for life in general, as he goes on to mention Goethe and Bulgakov, and elsewhere Hölderlin, Büchner, Virgil, Kleist, and Homer, among others, as figures who have mattered to him.

Unlike many film scholars, I approach Herzog's films not only from initial and sustained experiences of conviction in their achievements, but also out of a sense I share with him of the urgency of the problems of human life they address. As a result, this study is more personal and less diagnostic, skeptical, and driven by a counter-Herzogian politics of representation than many studies are. Of course some films strike me as less successful than others, often those such as *Queen of the Desert* (2015) or *Salt and Fire* (2016) that are comparatively more plot-driven than much of Herzog's work. Even here, however, there are entrancing images at moments—the salt desert in *Salt and Fire*, the Wadi Mujib Gorge in *Queen of the Desert*—that are worth thinking about, especially in relation to Herzog's work as a whole. At the same time, while more appreciative than skeptical, and prepared also to stay fairly close to Herzog's (often self-consciously stylized) self-presentations in his many written texts, conversations, and commentaries, my encounters with Herzog are also shaped by my having ready to hand a set of philosophical vocabularies (Freud, Heidegger, Merleau-Ponty, Schopenhauer, Nietzsche, Hegel, Cavell, and Benjamin) for engaging with Herzog's work. The result is a set of elaborations that set these philosophical vocabularies in mutual interaction with Herzog's work. The films as I read them do not merely illustrate one or another bit of philosophy. Instead they take up, develop, and worry at the problems of human life that motivate the philosophies, as the films think creatively and in images about exactly what these problems are and how to address them. They make various philosophical thoughts more plausible and available in experience, while at the same time modifying and inflecting them in various ways through images. In any case, there is no tenable ideal of perfect scientific exactness in the description of human life or filmic art. If we focus on nothing but movements of molecules, then agency and distinctively human life disappear from view. If a film's images were perfectly translated into an exact binary code (as happens in digital filmmaking) and that code then scrutinized for *its* significance, we would learn nothing. Film, like art in general and like human life, is made for attentive apprehension and emotional engagement.

What, then, are the problems of human life that Herzog's films take up? —One way to begin thinking about this question is to think about Freud's account of the impulses and powers that inform human life in general, impulses and powers that set up a constitutive tension between the irrepudiable pursuit of pleasure and its standing frustration. Herzog notoriously scorns psychoanalysis, remarking that "in its magnitude the catastrophe of psychoanalysis is comparable to the Spanish Inquisition. That is to say, the Inquisition wanted declarations of beliefs, and light shined into every last corner. They even wanted to weed out the Muslim elements that were still floating around, hiding in Spain. Psychoanalysis is exactly as bad."[1] While this remark may be aimed accurately enough at a conception of psychoanalysis according to which the analyst is a detached, perhaps violent, discoverer of hidden secrets through the use of expert techniques, it fails to touch more philosophically sophisticated alternative conceptions of psychoanalysis, such as that of Jonathan Lear, according to which the analyst helps to cultivate in the analysand the skill of hearing tensions and ambivalences that mark the analysand's life.[2] In any case, the idea that human life *is* marked by constitutive tensions can scarcely be plausibly denied. In *Civilization and Its Discontents*, the most culturally oriented statement of his mature philosophical anthropology, Freud offers his sharpest description of the constitutive tension between impulses that seek pleasure and the satisfying discharge of energy, on the one hand, and standing sources of frustration, on the other.

What do [human beings] demand of life and wish to achieve in it? The answer to this can hardly be in doubt. They strive after happiness; they want to become happy and to remain so. This endeavour has two sides, a positive and a negative aim. It aims, on the one hand, at an absence of pain and unpleasure, and, on the other, at the experiencing of strong feelings of pleasure. ... As we see, what decides the purpose of life is simply the programme of the pleasure principle. This principle dominates the operation of the mental apparatus from the start. There can be no doubt

---

[1]Herzog, in Katja Nicodemus, "Herr der Schmerzen," [Interview with Herzog], *Die Zeit* February 4, 2010, *Feuilleton*, 45; trans. Laurie Johnson, in "Werner Herzog's Romantic Spaces," in *A Companion to Werner Herzog*, ed. Brad Prager (Walden, MA: Wiley-Blackwell, 2012), pp. 510–27, at p. 522.

[2]See Jonathan Lear, *Therapeutic Action: An Earnest Plea for Irony* (New York: Other Press, 2003); Lear, *A Case for Irony* (Cambridge, MA: Harvard University Press, 2015).

about its efficacy, and yet its programme is at loggerheads with the whole world, with the macrocosm as much as with the microcosm. There is no possibility at all of its being carried through; all the regulations of the universe run counter to it.[3]

Freud goes on to list the sources of suffering that continuously frustrate the pursuit of happiness as one's own body with its liabilities to illness and breakdown, the hostile and dangerous external world, and frequently hostile, jealous, and competitive fellow human beings.[4] As available strategies for coping with these sources of suffering, Freud lists (i) intoxication, (ii) asceticism, (iii) sublimation in work, (iv) indulgence in art and fantasy, (v) reclusion, (vi) love, and (vii) the pursuit of beauty[5]—a fair enough list, where, unfortunately, no strategy offers much promise of continuous success. The pursuit of love in particular, according to Freud, is haunted by aggressive instincts and the general impossibility of loving one's neighbor.[6] Pleasure-seeking impulses, described as the affair of the id, continually bump up against the requirements and norms of common social life, themselves internalized as commands of the superego or agency of inhibition. "The price we pay for our advance in civilization," as Freud puts it, "is a loss of happiness through the heightening of the sense of guilt."[7] No human life is one perpetual progress, smooth and bright, and inhibition and unresolved antagonisms are the costs of living within the walls of society and of peace.

---

[3]Sigmund Freud, *Civilization and Its Discontents* [1930], trans. James Strachey (New York: W. W. Norton & Company, 2010), pp. 42–3.

[4]Ibid., p. 44.

[5]Ibid., pp. 45–53.

[6]Ibid., p. 91.

[7]Ibid., p. 131.

Perhaps worse yet, often enough people, and especially people in advanced industrial-consumer societies, undertake to navigate life's constitutive tensions inaptly, particularly when they primarily seek the practice-external goods of wealth and power, rather than enjoying the inherent goods that are internal to activities. Or as Freud puts it, "it is impossible to escape the impression that people commonly use false standards of measurement—that they seek power, success and wealth for themselves and admire them in others, and that they underestimate what is of true value in life."[8] Most consumer goods *are* goods, and, as Jon Elster remarks, "most consumption satisfies needs that no one need be ashamed of having,"[9] especially the more one's life is troubled by genuine scarcity. In addition, one should not underestimate the pluralized possibilities of life, the widened spheres of individual liberty with careers significantly open to talents, and the increased availability for many of relative freedom from desperate want that liberal and commercial modernity affords. Nonetheless, it is also difficult to avoid noticing the high incidences of vulgar egoistic-material competitiveness, low-grade depression, drift, and desperate escapism within advanced industrial-commercial life, as getting and spending we lay waste our powers.

Once upon a time, the terms of apt comportment in life were settled by tradition rooted in immediate necessities owing to scarcity. Authoritative accounts of these terms were provided by heroic literary traditions (Homer, the Icelandic Edda), by systematic philosophies rooted in comprehensive metaphysical cosmologies (Plato, Aristotle, Stoicism, Skepticism, Eudaimonism), or by religions. As Pierre Hadot

---

[8]Ibid., p. 23.
[9]Jon Elster, *An Introduction to Karl Marx* (Cambridge, England: Cambridge University Press, 1986), p. 51.

usefully characterizes the educational programs of the Ancient-Hellenistic philosophical schools:

> The individual was to be torn away from his habits and social prejudices, his way of life totally changed, and his way of looking at the world radically metamorphosed into a cosmic-"physical" perspective. … By ignoring unnatural and unnecessary desires, we can return to our original nucleus of freedom and independence, which may be defined by the satisfaction of natural and necessary desires. Thus, all spiritual exercises are, fundamentally, a return to the self, in which the self is liberated from the state of alienation into which it has been plunged by worries, passions, and desires. The "self" liberated in this way is no longer merely our egoistic, passionate individuality: it is our *moral* person, open to universality and objectivity, and participating in the universal nature of thought.[10]

Nowadays, however, these educational programs are evidently more or less authoritarian and epistemically untrustworthy. (How is one to know the Good, the conditions for the self-development of Noûs, or the will of God?) Hadot recommends a pluralistic recovery of the practices of the schools, in accordance with Seneca's dictum *toti se inserens mundi*—"plunging oneself into the totality of the world."[11] But exactly how to do this—with what courses of activity and life orientations in view, and based on which reasons—is the problem, a problem to which resoluteness, existentialist decisionism, and arbitrarily willed fundamentalism provide no satisfactory solutions.

---

[10]Pierre Hadot, *Philosophy as a Way of Life: Spiritual Exercises from Socrates to Foucault*, trans. Michael Chase (Malden, MA: Wiley-Blackwell, 1995), pp. 103–4.

[11]Ibid., pp. 209, 252, 273.

Despairing of the availability of any single systematic moral, political, and cultural system authoritatively rooted in a knowable cosmology, one might with John Rawls rest one's hopes in a pluralized, diverse just society that is informed by a sense of fairness.[12] The hope is, as Samuel Freeman puts it, that "the [Rawlsian] political conception [of justice] provides a public justification of liberal institutions that is 'freestanding,' hence based in fundamental ideals democratic citizens share in common, and independent of the comprehensive views that form an overlapping consensus."[13] Attractive though this suggestion is, it is also easy to worry that a sense of fairness can be colonized by instrumental reasoning, distorted by radical inequalities in holdings, and weakened and contested as a result of the disappearance of "overlapping consensus" about the general shape of fairness. As Fuat Gorsozlu pointedly puts it, "when unreasonable doctrines [stemming from either contested fundamentalisms or radical inequalities and resentments] grow so strong, it may be too late for the liberal democratic regime. ... [Normative stability requires] prevent[ing] the unreasonable from becoming strong enough to overwhelm the liberal political regime."[14] But how is one to do *that*, other than by arbitrary sheer suppression of one's opponents, once a shared authoritative sense of fairness

---

[12]In *A Theory of Justice,* a sense of fairness is one of the two distinctive "moral powers," along with the ability to articulate and live according to a conception of the good, that Rawls assumes human beings possess and whose exercise they take seriously in shaping their lives. See Rawls, *A Theory of Justice,* rev. ed. (Cambridge, MA: Harvard University Press, 1999). p. xii.

[13]Samuel Freeman, "Political Liberalism and the Possibility of a Just Constitution," *Chicago-Kent Law Review* 69, 3 (1994) *Symposium on John Rawls Political Liberalism,* pp. 619–68, at p. 668.

[14]Fuat Gorsozlu, "Political Liberalism and the Fate of Unreasonable People," *Touro Law Review* 30, 1 (2014), pp. 35–56, at p. 55.

is lost on the ground? In a modern, technologically developed, highly pluralized, inegalitarian economy, lack of consensus about either cosmological systems or political values is all too likely to yield education reduced to the development of skills needed by docile and reliable workers, ideological conceptions of freedom as escape and rich hedonistic consumption in the private sphere, empty clichés about the value of choice, and simmering instability, expressed in resentment, depression, fantasy, bluster, and reactive violence.

In this situation, in the absence of effective, attractive, alternative practices, consciousness-raising about human powers and interests is on its own liable to co-optation as another consumer good in the form of self-help nostrums. One needs courage, but in cathexis to meaningful activity, rather than as empty, avant-gardist provocation or jejune rule-breaking. One must somehow find a stance that yields meaningful orientation in life, in a self-sustaining way, against the grain of commercial and consumptive business as usual, but without the hubris of implausibly claiming privileged metaphysical knowledge.

Undertaking the work of this finding is the task and achievement of Herzog's films and practice of rogue filmmaking. As Herbert Golder, Herzog's sometime assistant director and co-writer, puts it:

> The miracle at the heart of [Herzog's] films is mankind's relentless struggle to find meaning, despite the indifference and hostility of the universe. However barren and parched the wasteland, however ice-encased and sheer the mountain, however fathomless the abyss, however dense and overgrown the jungle, the human spirit digs in, sends up its flare and ultimately—like Stroszek and his fireworks in *Signs of Life*, the existential flight of Walter Steiner, the scientists studying neutrinos in the upper atmosphere in *Encounters at the*

End of the World, the painters inside the Chauvet cave—writes its will across the sky in stars. The physical and metaphysical (the latter often arising in the fierce struggle to overcome the crushing gravity imposed by the former) are of a piece in Werner's work.[15]

In a speech given in Milan after a screening of *Lessons of Darkness* (1992), Herzog addresses directly the issue of the presence of the Absolute—the fundamental determining conditions of meaningful human life that might guide activity were we only somehow to grasp them—in his work.

> The Absolute, the Sublime, the Truth … What do these words mean? This is, I must confess, the first time in my life that I have sought to settle such questions outside of my work, which I understand, first and foremost, in practical terms. By way of qualification, I should add at once that I am not going to venture a definition of the Absolute, even if that concept casts its shadow over everything that I say here.
>
> … I can only very vaguely begin to fathom the Absolute; I am in no position to define the concept. For now, I'll stay on the trusted ground of praxis. Even if we cannot really grasp it, I would like to tell you about an unforgettable encounter I had with Truth while shooting *Fitzcarraldo*.
>
> … The inhabitants of the village of Shivakoreni were not sure whether it was true that on the other side of the Andes there was a monstrously large body of water, an ocean. In addition, there was the fact that this monstrous water, the Pacific, was supposedly salty.

---

[15]Herbert Golder, "Shooting on the Lam," in *Werner Herzog—A Guide for the Perplexed*, ed. Paul Cronin (London: Farrar, Straus, and Giroux, 2014), pp. 478–88, at p. 486.

We drove to a restaurant on the beach a little south of Lima to eat. But our two Indian delegates didn't order anything. They went silent and looked out over the breakers. They didn't approach the water, just stared at it. Then one asked for a bottle. I gave him my empty beer bottle. No, that wasn't right, it had to be a bottle that you could seal well. So I bought a bottle of cheap Chilean red, had it uncorked, and poured the wine out into the sand. We sent the bottle to the kitchen to be cleaned as carefully as possible. Then the men took the bottle and went, without a word, to the shoreline. Still wearing the new blue jeans, sneakers, and T-shirts that we had bought for them at the market, they waded in to the waves. They waded, looking over the expanse of the Pacific Ocean, until the water reached their underarms. Then, they took a taste of the water, filled the bottle and sealed it carefully with a cork. This bottle filled with water was their proof for the village that there really was an ocean. I asked cautiously whether it wasn't just a *part* of the truth. No, they said, if there is a bottle of seawater, then the whole ocean must be true as well.[16]

Here two things deserve particular notice. First, Herzog implies that he has sought to settle questions about the Absolute practically, within his work. Second, there is a truth—here called the truth of the ocean, elsewhere called ecstatic truth—a truth with which Herzog claims "an unforgettable encounter," and a truth that can be partially captured and conveyed to others, albeit obscurely, in a small bottle or in a film. This truth is a disclosure of something fundamental—the whole of nature, the self-development of the Absolute, the fact of the

---

[16]Werner Herzog, "On the Absolute, the Sublime, and Ecstatic Truth," trans. Moira Weigel, *Arion* 17, 3 (Winter 2010), pp. 1–12, at pp. 2, 3, 5.

ocean—that surrounds and shapes everything we do, but that fails to present itself within the orbit of business as usual. Hence Laurie Ruth Johnson's characterization of Herzog as in pursuit of "a knowledge [that is not] interesting only for its use value or directly convertible into profit, ... a non-instrumental knowledge" that requires an effort "to approximate metaphysical truth in a post-metaphysical age" is apt.[17]

What is sought is thus a fundamental orientation of our life within nature that cuts against the grains of profit-making and instrumentalist individual satisfaction. In *The Minnesota Declaration*, Herzog distinguishes between "a merely superficial truth, the truth of accountants" that remains within the sphere of instrumentalist business as usual and "poetic, ecstatic truth [that is] mysterious and elusive, and can be reached only through fabrication and imagination and stylization" (Cronin, 476). This latter, ecstatic truth requires, as Brad Prager puts it, "a standpoint outside of the everyday or the prosaic, ... a point outside of conventional rationality,"[18] and for Herzog it is essentially available perceptually, not verbally, or at any rate not in ordinarily verbal, non-poetic formulations. Herzog's pursuit of ecstatic, metaphysical, re-orienting truth in and through images involves what Prager calls a "distrust of language both as a means to represent the world and as a vessel to communicate meaning, ... [and] an elevation of the sensual, physical, and corporeal above the verbal."[19] Ecstatic truth requires Herzog to use the camera to find the adequate image, surrounded by narrative materials on

---

[17]Laurie Ruth Johnson, *Forgotten Dreams: Revisiting Romanticism in the Cinema of Werner Herzog* (Rochester, NY: Camden House, 2016), pp. 114, 149.

[18]Brad Prager, *The Cinema of Werner Herzog: Aesthetic Ecstasy and Truth* (London: Wallflower Press, 2007), p. 182.

[19]Ibid., pp. 3, 51.

which the image comments, and it requires us, the viewers, both to immerse ourselves in the image and to grasp its use as admonitory commentary on more ordinary, formula-governed human actions.

In an important recent study of German Romanticism, especially Schlegel, Fred Rush focuses on "subjectivity's relation to a ground that cannot be exhibited as such within the subjective domain" and on "the inability on the part of the subject to grasp ultimate meaning in the very act of trying to do so."[20] Like Herzog as well as Wordsworth and Hölderlin, Schlegel held that the best one could do is to develop an "inventory of practices for life under the conditions of the absence from experience of the absolute."[21] Even the notion of an inventory—a list one might consult—is arguably too strong, since any image or disclosive symbol through which one might undertake to grasp and present the absolute as a justifying ground for practice will itself be constitutively incomplete, insofar as it is marked by the subject's having only a particular finite point of view on the whole. Unlike philosophy that seeks fixed doctrines and *doxa*, poetry, along with art in general, including film, "is able to involve philosophical understanding," as Rush puts it, "while recognizing that the 'result' of the exercise of that understanding will not exhaust its object and should not even attempt to do so."[22] Poetry and art present at best incomplete and uncertain intimations of possibilities of fuller life, while ending in cadences and forms of closure that involve only temporary and temporalized diminishings of a sense of outsiderliness and anxiety. To pursue or to insist on stronger, doctrinal conclusions is the time- and finitude-denying path of narcissism and madness.

---

[20]Fred Rush, *Irony and Idealism: Rereading Schlegel, Hegel, and Kierkegaard* (Oxford: Oxford University Press, 2016), p. 66.

[21]Ibid., p. 39.

[22]Ibid., p. 55.

Yet quietism is not an available option either, at least for anyone who is prone even to moments of reflection and anxiety-inducing detachment from the stream of life. In Rush's formulation, "one *should* answer the vocation of one's discursive subjectivity and pursue in the most vigorous way the constructive activity of subjects relative to the world that Schlegel … takes to be definitive of subjects."[23] In doing so, the best one might hope for is not arrival at a fixed doctrine, but rather what Schlegel calls *Wechselerweis*—a good enough but not completely closed proving of oneself to oneself in practice, as when one shows oneself within doing to be "good enough" at being a cook or tennis player, parent or writer, spouse or co-worker or colleague, so that one's anxiety is stilled for a time in how one occupies a particular finite role.[24]

Operating within the orbit of suspicion of doctrinal solutions to the problems of contemporary life, there can be for Herzog no useful standing themes of success that plots can repeatedly simply illustrate. Instead, in order for him to get started, as in the Wordsworthian trope of the halted traveler, some person, scene, event, or image must arrest his gaze and demand capture on film. *Signs of Life* (1968), Herzog's first feature, was significantly provoked by his sighting of the valley of the 10,000 rotating windmills on Crete (Cronin, 49–50); *Encounters at the End of the World* (2007) was initiated by his seeing Henry Kaiser's underwater footage of the caverns and pillars of ice beneath the Antarctic shelf (Cronin, 381); *Grizzly Man* (2005) by his encounter with Timothy Treadwell's raw footage (Cronin, 368). Herzog is famous for shooting images that lie at the heart of his films that can be captured in only one (highly planned) take: the opening

---

[23]Ibid., p. 45.
[24]See ibid., p. 43.

shot in *Aguirre* of the descent of the expedition into the jungle from the top of the Andes (Cronin, 109); the hauling of the ship over the mountains in *Fitzcarraldo* (1982). Verbal tropes such as "I knew instantly that ... ," "it was instantly clear that ... ," and "I knew immediately that ..." recur frequently in his reflections on his work in his conversations with Paul Cronin in describing moments either in which an image in life demands filmic capture or in which a shot has been perfectly accomplished. The result of Herzog's captivation by the image and its capture, both in individual films and across Herzog's oeuvre, is what the film scholar Daniel Yacavone usefully describes as Herzog's film world: not only

> the fictional reality or story-world abstracted from a film's formal and medial presentation, [but] also ... that presentation itself, making use of the properties and possibilities of cinema—entailing camera movements, color schemes, rhythms, editing styles, music, production design, performance registers, soundscapes, and so on—as all contributing to the creation and experience of a readily identifiable cinematic world as a perceptual-imaginative and affective whole.[25]

A few moments of almost any Herzog film are enough for most viewers with minimal acquaintance with his work to establish that the film bears his characteristic stylistic signatures—long takes of sensuous landscapes, 360 degree pans, liturgical scores, either excessive or radically minimal acting—that here is an instance of Herzog's world or Herzog's "artistic vision of human experiential reality [presented] on integrated sensory, affective, and cognitive levels."[26] Though not at all clearly present in all filmmakers, there

---

[25]Daniel Yacavone, *Film Worlds* (New York: Columbia University Press, 2015), pp. 7–8.
[26]Ibid., p. 267.

clearly *is* emphatically present in Herzog's films an extraordinary "extranarrative symbolization (exemplification [of the actual world, captured on film]) [that], while copresent with denotation [the presented narrative story-world] transcends and stands out from it and the represented diegetic world."[27]

The central point of the emphatic, stylized presentation of the actual world on film is, for Herzog, the disclosure of possibilities of meaningful life in nature and their fateful inhibition. Herzog uses the Heideggerian term *alêtheia*—truth as disclosure—to describe the magical possibilities of truth presentation that pertain to movies as such:

> The Greek word for truth, *alêtheia*, [is not] simple to grasp. Etymologically speaking, it comes from the verb *lanthanein*, "to hide," and the related word *lêthos*, "the hidden," "the concealed." *Alêtheia* is, therefore, a form of negation, a negative definition: it is the "not-hidden," the revealed, the truth. Thinking through language [*im sprachlichen Denken*], the Greeks meant, therefore, to define truth as an act of disclosure—a gesture related to the cinema, where an object is set into the light and then a latent, not yet visible image is conjured onto celluloid, where it first must be developed, then disclosed.[28]

Here Herzog, who studied Greek in his classical humanistic Gymnasium and who continues to read Homer in Greek, is directly drawing on Heidegger's discussion of truth as unconcealment (*alêtheia*) as the characteristic function and achievement of important art, in his "The Origin of the Work of Art." In important art, as Heidegger puts it, an "entity emerges into the unconcealedness of

---

[27]Ibid., p. 123.
[28]Herzog, "On the Absolute, the Sublime, and Ecstatic Truth," p. 11.

its being. The Greeks called the unconcealedness of beings *alêtheia.*
... This opening up, i.e. this deconcealing, i.e. the truth of beings,
happens in the work. In the art work, the truth of what is has set itself
to work."[29] Truth here is not a matter of copying, simply recognizable
description or depiction, or correspondence—what Heidegger
calls truth as *adequatio*: recognition-enabling fit between sign
and object—but rather of coming to an orientation for and within
worldly practice, in and through one's encounter with the work and
what it presents. One is lifted by the encounter with the work out of
confusion, half-heartedness, and stupor and into clarity, resoluteness,
and a sense of how things matter in and for one's life. Arriving at
such a stance is altogether different from occupying a spectatorial-
theoretical stance, where the task is either to cut through, abstract
from, and ignore emotions, moods, and secondary qualities in order
to get to a measurable material essence or simply to have an enjoyable
experience.[30] Instead, one arrives at a knowing that is a willing—a
wholehearted and apt immersion in the unfolding of Being, as in
Seneca's *toti se inserens mundi.* Or as Heidegger puts it:

> He who truly knows what is, knows what he wills to do in the midst
> of what is. ... Knowing that remains a willing, and willing that
> remains a knowing, is the existing human being's entrance into and
> compliance with the unconcealedness of Being. The resoluteness
> [*Entschlossenheit*] intended in *Being and Time* is not the deliberate
> action of a subject, but the opening up of human being, out of its
> captivity in that which is, to the openness of Being.[31]

---

[29]Martin Heidegger, "The Origin of the Work of Art," trans. Albert Hofstadter, in *Poetry, Language, Thought* (New York: Harper & Row, 1971), pp. 18–86, at pp. 35, 38.

[30]"Experience is the source that is [typically] standard not only for art appreciation and enjoyment, but also for artistic creation. Everything is an experience. Yet perhaps experience is the element in which art dies." Ibid., p. 77.

[31]Ibid., p. 65.

This is no doubt more than a little obscure, especially if one lacks a substantial and reliable cosmology that includes an account of apt human life. Heidegger's own accounts in *Being and Time* of the achievement of resoluteness are distressingly empty and hence open to ready appropriation by decisionist fascism. "But on what basis does Dasein [human life] disclose itself in resoluteness? On what is it to resolve? *Only* the resolution itself can give the answer."[32] Heidegger's later talk of patiently hearkening poetically to the call of Being and, worse yet, of "the nation … return[ing] to itself for the fulfillment of its vocation" and of "simple and essential decisions in the destiny of an historical people"[33] is scarcely any better.

Whatever difficulties trouble his account of meaningful life, however, Heidegger's formulations of the problems that haunt life in modern industrial-commercial societies have considerable resonance. In *Being and Time*, he describes modern life as more or less typically characterized by "'fallenness' into the 'world' [as] an absorption in Being-with-one-another, insofar as the latter is guided by idle talk, curiosity, and ambiguity," and resulting in "anxiety" and a sense of "uncanny floating," as one feels always already involved with the world, but without conviction in the significance of what one does.[34] Within this fallenness, life is characterized by "inauthenticity and failure to stand by one's self," as "Dasein maintains itself proximally and for the most part in the deficient modes of solicitude."[35] In not knowing how to care effectively either for oneself or for others, not knowing how to maintain well-founded conviction, evident in action, in individual and joint social life,

---

[32] Martin Heidegger, *Being and Time* [1927], trans. John Macquarrie and Edward Robinson (Oxford: Blackwell, 1962), p. 345.
[33] Heidegger, "The Origin of the Work of Art," pp. 41, 47.
[34] Heidegger, *Being and Time*, pp. 214, 220, 233.
[35] Ibid., pp. 158, 166.

the real dictatorship of the "they" is unfolded. We take pleasure in and enjoy ourselves as *they* take pleasure; we read, see, and judge about literature and art as *they* see and judge; likewise we shrink back from the "great mass" as *they* shrink back; we find "shocking" what *they* find shocking. The "they," which is nothing definite, and which all are, though not as the sum, prescribes the kind of Being of everydayness.[36]

Crowd-sourcing, big data, re-tweets, Facebook likes, memes, internet "challenges," numbers of followers, "you may like," celebrity culture—all these are but the most recent symptoms of a deep-rooted lack of conviction in who one is and what one does.

Herzog maintains if anything an even sharper sense of the problem of fallen, average everydayness, under the heading of "the assault of virtual reality."

From then on, what constitutes truth—or, to put it in much simpler form, what constitutes *reality*—became a greater mystery to me than it had been. The two intervening decades have posed unprecedented challenges to our concept of reality.

When I speak of assaults on our understanding of reality, I am referring to new technologies that, in the past twenty years, have become general articles of everyday use: the digital special effects that create new and imaginary realities in the cinema. It's not that I want to demonize these technologies; they have allowed the human imagination to accomplish great things—for instance, reanimating dinosaurs convincingly on screen. But, when we consider all the possible forms of virtual reality that have become part of everyday life—in the Internet, in video games, and on reality TV; sometimes also in strange

---

[36]Ibid., p. 164.

mixed forms—the question of what "real" reality is poses itself constantly afresh.

What is *really* going on in the reality TV show *Survivor*? Can we ever really trust a photograph, now that we know how easily everything can be faked with Photoshop? Will we ever be able to completely trust an email, when our twelve-year-old children can show us that what we're seeing is probably an attempt to steal our identity, or perhaps a virus, a worm, or a "Trojan" that has wandered into our midst and adopted every one of our characteristics? Do I already exist somewhere, cloned, as many *Doppelgänger*, without knowing anything about it?[37]

Here the assault on virtual reality is, for Herzog, both source and symptom of captivation by fallen, average everydayness, as we live amid simulacra, without real engagement with the material world or one another, and without conviction in what we do and how we live.

Just as with Heidegger, Herzog's filmic responses to the problem of fallen, average everydayness have frequently been charged with fascist decisionism and regressivism. Here are just a few of the most pointed of these charges:

[Herzog] creates a romantic, allegorical universe which excites the eye and threatens to muffle the mind.[38]

[Herzog is] the exponent of a neo-romantic regression … [who indulges in] poetic reductionism … [and adopts] a fundamentally premodern perspective.[39]

---

[37]Herzog, "On the Absolute, the Sublime, and Ecstatic Truth," p. 5.

[38]Robert Philip Kolker, *The Altering Eye: Contemporary International Cinema* (Cambridge, England: Open Book Publishers, 1983), p. 267.

[39]Gertrud Koch, "Blindness as Insight: *Land of Silence and Darkness*," in *The Films of Werner Herzog: Between Mirage and History*, ed. Timothy Corrigan (London: Routledge, 1986), pp. 73–86, at pp. 75, 79–80.

Herzog's insistence on the primacy of the symbolic over actual human life, coupled with an aestheticization of death, mark him as dangerously close to fascistic tendencies. The prophet-artist is driven by a mystical need to create, regardless of the damage caused to others, simply because a genius is supposedly at work, ... as a director militantly at odds with the values and morals of bourgeois society.[40]

Throughout the 1970s and 1980s, Werner Herzog was often seen as a director attempting to translate Richard Wagner's concept of the "total work of art" (*Gesamtkunstwerk*) into the realm of German auteur cinema. According to this understanding, Herzog not only sought to turn the world into an aesthetic spectacle, but also to overwhelm his spectators with monumental gestures and grandiose visions. Recalling Wagner's stress on mystical totality, Herzog was said to dissolve the boundaries of the aesthetic, to replace social engagement with romantic excess, and to redefine the sublime as a site of irrational transcendence and individual redemption. Like Wagner's monumental operas, Herzog's art—it was concluded—resulted in no less than a precarious aestheticization of life. It invalidated ethical or political considerations, and it approached the world as if it were grand opera itself, a universe solely designed for dramatic expressions of empathy and perverse self-sacrifice.[41]

In general, the criticism is that Herzog, via his excessive aesthetic stylizations in his films, avoids actual history, especially real political

---

[40]Jan-Christopher Horak, "W. H., or the Mysteries of Walking in Ice," in ibid., pp. 25–49, at pp. 31, 38–9.

[41]Lutz Koepnick, "Archetypes of Emotion: Werner Herzog and Opera," in Prager, ed. *A Companion to Werner Herzog* (Oxford: Wiley-Blackwell, 2012), pp. 149–67, at p. 149, summarizing criticisms with which he disagrees and to which he offers a reply.

and social history, and has no sense of ordinary life: he attempts to forward via symbolization a premodern salvation myth that makes no contact with life as it is actually lived.

There is some measure of truth in these charges. Herzog does not pay much attention to either ordinary domestic life in advanced societies or to institutional politics, and, as Hegel sees clearly, one should not underemphasize the importance of family life, workplace identity, and political citizenship for meaningful life, at least when familial, economic, and political institutions work well. (Herzog himself indicates a late recognition of the importance of family life, arrived at partly through the making of *Into the Abyss* [2011] [Cronin, 425].) Evidently, however, these institutions do not always work well. Nor do we have clear and convincing pictures from either the left or the right of what family, economic, and political life might look like in a productive way as a result of radical structural change rather than reform. Many people do find meaning in their lives to considerable extents precisely through participation in these flawed-enough but still fruitful institutions. More specifically, as Roger Hillman notes, it is true that "Herzog's films are not notable for their well-wrought narratives, nor for their subtle psychological portraits of expressive individuals (especially females). He often deprives characters of speech, and instead imposes a voice-over in which the voice is frequently his own."[42] When Herzog does come closer to making genre films such as the police procedural *Bad Lieutenant: Port of Call—New Orleans* (2009) or the historical sagas *Queen of the Desert* (2015) and *Invincible* (2001), the results are frequently disappointing. Herzog's predilection for what Deleuze calls the time-image over the movement-image and continuity editing often make it difficult for

---

[42]Roger Hillman, "Coming to Our Senses: The Viewer and Herzog's Sonic Worlds," in *A Companion to Werner Herzog*, ed. Prager, pp. 168–86, at p. 168.

him to track and represent dramatic action in more or less standard social terms.

But as Deleuze remarks, "Herzog sets out the greatest crystal-images in the history of cinema"[43] in *Heart of Glass* (1976), and in general his films, both fictional and documentary—the boundaries are deliberately unclear   are structured more like the Romantic poetry of arrest by an image, scene, person, or incident and its subsequent working through than they are by preconceived plot forms. As Lutz Koepnick puts it, defending Herzog's lyrical imagism, Herzog sets about "finding in the midst of perceptions of differences—the idiosyncrasies of the aesthetic—that which allows us to set frozen history in motion again. … [He] challenges the observer to perceive both the world and themselves in a new way, to (re)discover new ways of perception through unexpected experiences of motion and affect."[44] Such uncoverings of new possibilities of perception that may be experienced and shared in viewers' engagements with the filmic image may open up senses of enchantment, acknowledgment of temporality, awe, dismay, and horror that may themselves play fruitful, renovating roles in our attentions to institutional circumstances and more prosaic life. Should senses of beauty, disgust, awe, and difference *not* figure in how we act and engage with one another within our family, economic, and political lives? What would familial, economic, and political life be other than repressive stasis if there were no place in it for such experiences? Or, again in Koepnick's terms, Herzog's lyrical imagism

> encourages non-instrumental relationships between perception and (the) perceiving body based, not on desires to control, contain, and frame, but on our yearning to learn how to listen and let go, to

---

[43]Gilles Deleuze, Cinema 2: The Time Image, trans. Hugh Tomlinson and Robert Galeta (London: Continuum, 1989), p. 73.
[44]Koepnick, "Archetypes of Emotion," p. 163.

open ourselves up to what is contingent and beyond our control, … [calling into play] our ability to suspend linear temporal and spatial orders and—like a dreamer—experience the world of our perception as something beautifully ambivalent, enigmatic, in flux, inassimilable, and unpredictable.[45]

Given the prose of the world—our fallenness into average everydayness, whatever its unavoidable and enabling features—we stand in need of such openings.

Like Heidegger and Herzog, Maurice Merleau-Ponty insists that our being, as individual humans capable of reflection, occurs always already within nature and within historical worlds.

Since … we are in and toward the world, and since even our reflections take place in the temporal flow that they are attempting to capture (since they *sich einströmen* [flow along therein], as Husserl says), there is no thought that encompasses all of our thought. … The unity of the world, prior to being posited by knowledge through an explicit act of identification, is lived as already accomplished or as already there.[46]

There is no transcendental standpoint, no cosmic exile, from which the Absolute might be discursively grasped and the conditions of meaningful life perfectly discovered. We live within an unfolding whole of history-in-nature, and we stand in need of more adequate orientation. Merleau-Ponty explicitly opposes "the *aseity*

---

[45]Lutz Koepnick, "Herzog's Cave: On Cinema's Unclaimed Past and Forgotten Futures," *Germanic Review: Literature, Culture, Theory* 88, 3 (2013), pp. 271–85, at pp. 273, 283–4. Koepnick's formulation here suggests an interesting point of comparison between Herzog and Sam Mendes's *American Beauty* (1999), with its signature motif of the trash bag blowing in the wind.

[46]Maurice Merleau-Ponty, *Phenomenology of Perception*, trans. Donald A. Landes (New York: Routledge, 2012), pp. lxxviii, lxxxi.

[independent existence] of things" as fixed, external objects of contemplation, sensualism (the thought that our grasps of things reduce to flows of unstructured sensation), and idealism (the thought that our thinking is independent of history-in-nature, somehow occurring in a place apart).[47] "Phenomenology"—Merleau-Ponty's mode of philosophizing—"recognizes my thought as an inalienable fact and it eliminates all forms of idealism by revealing me as 'being in the world.'"[48] And yet, again as in Heidegger and Herzog, we can and must arrive at orientation, come to grips with our being in the world, so as to overcome drift, anomie, and depression within average everydayness. "We must—precisely in order to see the world and to grasp it as a paradox—rupture our familiarity with it, and this rupture can teach us nothing except the unmotivated springing forth of the world."[49] According to Merleau-Ponty, this rupture is to be accomplished by engaged, perceptual reflection that is not fully under conscious, agentive control.

> Reflection does not withdraw from the world toward the unity of consciousness as the foundation of the world; rather, it steps back in order to see transcendences spring forth and it loosens the intentional [i.e. subject-act guided] threads that connect us to the world in order to make them appear; it alone is conscious of the world because it reveals the world as strange and paradoxical.[50]

But what is engaged, perceptual reflection, and how does it rupture our familiarity with the world, enable us to see the world and grasp it as a paradox, disclose the unmotivated springing forth of the world, and

---

[47]Ibid., p. lxxix.
[48]Ibid., p. lxxvii.
[49]Ibid.
[50]Ibid.

reveal the world as strange and paradoxical? Merleau-Ponty argues that this engaged, perceptual reflection is accomplished in the haptically visual paintings of Cézanne and that we as viewers might share in this accomplishment, if we learn to engage with these paintings aright, seeing them as world-disclosures, not merely pleasing artifacts. An image, with a visible surface to be explored imaginatively, where this visible surface is itself an imaginative exploration of the unfolding world from a bodily standpoint—not any simple visual sensation having to do with the eye alone, and not any detached thought—is, for Merleau-Ponty, the key to achieving a sense of fuller orientation within a whole and more adequate involvement with it.

I know that I have the ability to articulate images that sit deeply inside us, that I can make them visible.[51]

—WERNER HERZOG, 1975

What Merleau-Ponty finds in Cézanne—an achievement of orienting disclosure, via the production of a markedly bodily situated visual image in which an audience can share—is exactly what Herzog aims at and accomplishes in his films—coupled with motion and a wider range of subject matters. Like Cézanne (as understood by Merleau-Ponty), Herzog constructs his images by beginning from a pronounced sense of bodily placement in relation to objects on which the camera is to focus, a sense of bodily placement that he traces in part to his physical involvements with ski jumping and soccer.

And athletics is something that I have been involved with *all* my life. I've always been a ski jumper and a soccer player, and yet, when

---

[51]Herzog, cited in J. Hoberman, "Obscure Objects of Desire," *Village Voice*, February 19, 1975, p. 61.

I work on a film, people always seem to think that this kind of work is just the result of some sort of an abstract academic concept of story development or some purely intellectual theory as to how drama should work. They don't seem to realize *all* that is involved in making a film. ... To give you a specific example of this process, in *Kaspar Hauser*, in order to set up the scene with the deathbed, really all that we had to do was to move the bed to the center of the room and very quickly arrange six or seven people so that they would just be standing or sitting around it, but now, when I see this scene in the film, I realized that it is a *perfectly* balanced image, and yet it only took me five seconds to do it! I just had all these people there, and I said, "You sit here, you stand there, you stand there, you sit here," and that was it! It was just a *physical knowledge* which I was able to possess of a certain order that existed within that space, and it is that kind of knowledge which has decided many an important battle for me.[52]

And, as in Cézanne, the images that are produced are to be entered imaginatively, as devices for the viewer's exploration of the world, as that world is suffused with objects of emotional significance. They are neither records of Herzog's experience alone, nor depictions of what is simply given apart from human experience, imagination, and desire, but instead collective dream images of encountered meaning. "All these dreams are yours as well, and the only distinction between me and you is that I can articulate them."[53] We are to see significance in them imaginatively and emotionally, directing our attention both to the image and to the meaning in the world that it discloses. In *Encounters at the End of the World* (2007), Herzog tells us that he

---

[52]Werner Herzog, "Images at the Horizon" (Interview, 1979), in *Herzog by Ebert*, ed. Roger Ebert (Chicago, IL: University of Chicago Press, 2017), pp. 3–48, at pp. 37–8.

[53]Herzog, *Burden of Dreams*, dir. Les Blank (El Cerrito, CA: Flower Films, 1982).

noticed that the divers [preparing to go underneath the Antarctic ice] in their routine were not speaking at all. To me, they were like priests preparing for mass. Under the ice the divers find themselves in a separate reality where space and time acquire a strange new dimension. Those few who have experienced the world under the frozen sky often speak of it as going down into the cathedral.

Herzog's films, too, similarly give us access to a separate reality where space and time acquire a strange new dimension. After this observation, we see 4:20 of extraordinary images of undersea creatures, divers' bubbles ascending toward an escape hole, floating jellyfish, and an underwater valley of clams, surrounded by ice cliffs, all backed by a choir singing the Bulgarian folk song/chant "Planino stara planino mari" (Old mountain, I have often wandered about you).

As in Wordsworth halted on a journey by a disclosive spot of time, or Hölderlin halted on the bridge in Heidelberg or outside Bordeaux at the confluence of the Dordogne and Garonne, a moment of experience that carries collective disclosive significance is captured lyrically, here in images rather than in words. Herzog describes the initiating experience of *Signs of Life* in exactly these Wordsworthian-Hölderlinian terms:

> While in Greece, riding a donkey on Crete, I stumbled across the Lasithi Plateau. I was travelling over a mountain pass and looked down into a valley. Beneath me lay ten thousand revolving windmills; it was a field of spinning flowers gone mad. The squeaking noise alone was astonishing. My heart stood still and I had to sit down. "I have either gone insane or seen something very significant," I said to myself. It turned out these frenzied windmills were real, pumping water for irrigation. I knew as soon as I stood there I would return one day to make a film, and years later this cosmic image became a pivotal one in *Signs of Life*. My attention

has always been drawn to the screams that emanate from certain images, and if something cries out so loudly and insistently, I respond. Had I never seen the windmills, I wouldn't have made the connection between this unimaginable ecstatic landscape and the von Arnim story, which I read later on. (Cronin, 49–50)

As Wordsworth has it in *The Prelude*, "There are in our existence spots of time, /That with distinct pre-eminence retain /A renovating virtue, whence—depressed /By false opinion and contentious thought, /Or aught of heavier or more deadly weight, /In trivial occupations, and the round /Of ordinary intercourse—our minds /Are nourished and invisibly repaired."[54] Herzog describes the significance of the windmill image in *Signs of Life* in similarly Wordsworthian terms of

Figure 1 *The field of rotating windmills, from* Signs of Life *(1968).*

[54]William Wordsworth, *The Prelude* [1850], in Wordsworth, *Selected Poems and Prefaces*, ed. Jack Stillinger (Boston, MA: Houghton-Mifflin, 1965), Book X, ll. 208–15, p. 345.

arrest and absorption that pull one out of the ways of the world and into something mysteriously significant.

> These kinds of shot are where the film holds its breath. They feel as mystifying and intense to me as to any other spectator, and I am convinced it is moments like these that truly decide my films. They are the places where the various threads suddenly run together to form a knot. They propel the plot forwards, even though I do not really know how.[55]

Importantly, the images that mysteriously disclose significance in absorbed attention to them are images of real things, not products only of the director's constructive imagination. Herzog notoriously scorns the use of special effects, and he emphasizes the importance of the camera's focus on things that really happen, in order to make what he calls "movie movies" as opposed to more artificial constructions. "Porno movies are movie movies. Karate films are movie movies. Fred Astaire films are movie movies."[56] The ship must actually be hauled over the mountain and sent down the rapids (*Fitzcarraldo*, 1982). The enormous stones in *Invincible* (2001) must be lifted by an authentic strongman, Steiner must actually ski-jump, fall, and set a world record (*The Great Ecstasy of the Woodcarver Steiner* [1973]), Huie must actually preach (*Huie's Sermon* [1980]), and the auctioneers must actually sell cattle and compete with each other (*How Much Wood Would a Woodchuck Chuck* [1976]).

---

[55]Herzog, *Herzog on Herzog*, ed. Paul Cronin (New York: Farrar, Straus, and Giroux, 2002), p. 80. Herzog uses the same tropes of held breath and threads forming a knot to describe the extended shot of the rapids of the Rio Urubamba in *Aguirre* (Cronin, p. 95).

[56]Herzog, in "Werner Herzog, 2004," Interview with Doug Aiken, *Index Magazine*, archived at http://www.indexmagazine.com/interviews/werner_herzog.shtml. Compare a similar, more extended passage at Cronin, p. 146.

As Noël Carroll aptly observes, Herzog, along with Terry Malick and Stan Brakhage, belongs to a group of filmmakers who are "concerned to acknowledge or to disclose the often ignored richness that is nevertheless believed to be always available to experience. These filmmakers share an advocacy of the immediacy of experience, that is, an avowal of the possibility of experience—or, at least, of dimensions of experience—independent from routine, social modes of schematization."[57] Herzog in particular achieves "emphasis on the optical" using long takes where "the composition has no center of interest," and "by emphasizing clouds and mists he foregrounds the lighting and opticality of scenes rather than their object-properties. The secondary qualities of scenes, rather than their primary qualities, are stressed."[58] The richness and absorbing character of visual experience is frequently contrasted with "language, which, in turn, is associated with practical and instrumental reason, with science and bureaucracy, with religion and civil society. ... Throughout Herzog's work, figures of public authority are portrayed as agents of specialized languages—languages often of instrumental knowledge and, therefore, languages connected with the exercise of power."[59] Such figures of coercive public authority include, among others, the commandant in *Woyzeck*, Van Helsing in *Nosferatu*, the priest Caraval in *Aguirre*, and the scribe in *Kaspar Hauser*.

Carroll goes on to worry that Herzog risks falling into mannerism when the devices of optical emphasis are used repeatedly. As a result of repetition, we may come to see these images primarily *as* Herzogian images—signature stylistic constructs—rather than as revelations of

---

[57]Noël Carroll, "Herzog, Presence, and Paradox," in *Interpreting the Moving Image*, ed. Carroll (Cambridge, England: Cambridge University Press, 1998), pp. 284–99, at p. 284.
[58]Ibid., pp. 295, 296.
[59]Ibid., p. 288.

a mysterious larger reality around us. "In vouching for something ineffable—in pointing it out and symbolizing it distinctly—Herzog makes those dimensions and properties of experience that he champions more and more effable."[60] Whether this is true, however, will depend on just how varied and plot-context specific these images are, as well as on what phenomena that support emphatic opticality the world continues to make available to the camera. Here the range of images that the world *has* made available and that Herzog has captured is astonishingly wide, from the windmills on Crete in *Signs of Life* (1968) and the Saharan desert of *Fata Morgana* (1970) to the blowing grasses of *Grizzly Man* (2005), the underwater sea-life and ice-chimneys of *Encounters at the End of the World* (2007), the caves of Chauvet of *Cave of Forgotten Dreams* (2010), the salt fields of *Salt and Fire* (2016), and all their cousins in between.

Contesting a reading of Herzog as committed to emphatic opticality or a visual sublime, Alan Singer has argued that:

It is indeed tempting to see Herzog as the mystic seer of sublime intuitions, since his mise-en-scène is always most compelling insofar as it seems to represent more than it can show: a ravishing white water cataract is revealed to be a flow of clouds through Bavarian mountain valleys (*Heart of Glass*); a figure animated by heat waves teases the camera with a point of focus it can approach only as a distortion (*Fata Morgana*); a telephoto collapsing of space renders the descent of a line of Pizarro's soldiers from an Amazonian mountaintop as a static infinity of space (*Aguirre*). … [Nonetheless, however] Herzog's mystic worlds finally always reveal the conditions of their viewing as their most oracular truth.[61]

---

[60]Ibid., p. 298.

[61]Alan Singer, "Comprehending Appearances: Werner Herzog's Ironic Sublime," in *The Films of Werner Herzog*, ed. Corrigan (London: Routledge, 1986), pp. 183–205, at p. 184.

That is, according to Singer, instead of bringing the viewer into rapt absorption in what is visually presented, Herzog characteristically makes us aware of the fact that we are viewing constructed images, insofar as he markedly emphasizes the use of tracking shots, intrusions of the camera into the image in some of the documentaries, insertions of archival footage, and shots from unusual points of view, such as 360-degree helicopter pans. In the end, according to Singer, the prima facie visually sublime images "resolutely return the viewer to contemplation of the representational devices that reveal them rather than to the putative world of visionary transcendence that would enfold them."[62]

There is something right about this, in that our attention *can* be held by how the image has been constructed as well as by what it presents. In this respect, Herzog's images afford a pronounced experience of what Richard Wollheim characterizes as twofoldness[63]: at the same time we hold in awareness both what is presented and the surface qualities of the presentation itself. In being aware of the constructed surface, moreover, we are further aware that it embodies the attentiveness and emotional-tonal involvement of a painterly or directorial gaze. Thus by engaging with the image, we can enter imaginatively into this involvement by sharing in its point of view. In general, in seeing we experience more—constructed surface, emotion, and mood—than the depicted object alone. As Thomas Elsaesser aptly notes, Herzog's distrust of narrative and pursuit of the image "has itself to do with the question of signification in the cinema, and the extent to which any logic of the [linguistic] signifier—whether narrative, causal, psychological or formal—dematerializes the image

---

[62]Ibid., p. 194.

[63]Richard Wollheim, *Painting as an Art* (Princeton, NJ: Princeton University Press, 1980), pp. 48–60.

[and all *it* can show and enable us to experience] on the side of the referent, while effectively excluding the subject from discourse."[64] Hence Singer goes too far in claiming that our awareness of the character of the construction occludes awareness of what it presents. Just as Wollheim claims, both forms of awareness are aspects of the same experience, and the image retains its emphatically optical quality. The overwhelming evidence of the striking images themselves is that Herzog is aiming seriously at disclosure, not irony about filmmaking. We stand in need, according to Herzog, of re-animating images. As he remarks about the use of hypnosis in *Heart of Glass* (1976), "One purpose ... was to discover to what extent it would be possible to bring out and emphasize those 'poetic' visionary qualities that are hidden inside so many people,"[65] precisely because poetic visions are needed in order to disclose possibilities of significance in life within the framework of contemporary industrial-commercial culture.

Though there is a continuing commitment on Herzog's part to emphatically optical capturing of the real, it is also important that the images captured *are* plot-context specific. The films are edited in order to make the images work effectively in their specific places in their respective films.

> One should never attempt to define this process *just* in terms of the images that you see on the screen, because it also involves a new form of "emotionality" which somehow underlies the images in *all* these films. For example, if all of you had not seen *Land of Silence and Darkness* and if I were to show you only the last five minutes of the film—the scene where there's a man who embraces a tree—all of you would probably think, "Well, there's a man who embraces a

---

[64]Thomas Elsaesser, "An Anthropologist's Eye: *Where the Green Ants Dream*," in *The Films of Werner Herzog*, ed. Corrigan (London: Methuen, 1986), pp. 133–56, at p. 148.

[65]Herzog, "Images at the Horizon," p. 24.

tree," and that's all. What's happening is really very simple; you just see a man who feels and embraces a tree, and that *is* all, but, if you had seen the *entire* film, then you would have received this scene and this image with a different dimension of depth and insight. It requires that additional one and a half hours of film preceding this scene to make you receptive and sensitive enough to be able to understand that this is one of the deepest moments you can ever encounter in the cinema.[66]

Films, after all, are not still photographs (whatever *their* powers), and Herzog is powerfully aware of and exploits all the devices of cinematic motion and editing, including extended traveling shots, pans, and cuts. (Interestingly, zooms are relatively less prominent in Herzog's work as he generally prefers to keep the overall spatial

Figure 2 *Herr Fleischmann explores a tree, from* Land of Silence and Darkness *(1971).*

[66]Ibid., pp. 24–5.

relations among the elements of a single scene steadily established.) Not *just* the images matter, but also their timings and sequencings in their specific contexts. As Wolfgang Ruf puts it with respect to *Land of Silence and Darkness* (1971), "in the editing of these images, in the carefully thought-out pans and tracking shots, a world becomes perceptible [*spürbar*], a world that is incongruent with that of our own, but one that by means of its very existence points to the delicate state of our self-image, beginning with our shared possibilities of communication."[67]

Not all images, however, are part of a smooth flow that supports continuous absorption. Some are deliberately interruptive and set in contrast to the ecstatic opticalities of nature. Stefanie Harris aptly notes a distinction between two kinds of photographic images that appear in *Even Dwarfs Started Small* (1970): images that depict confinement or restriction and images that unfold in a continuous flow. *Even Dwarfs* opens with a shot of Hombre, a principal among the rioting dwarfs, now re-institutionalized post-riot, with the narrative of the rebellion then shown in extended flashback.

> With the images of the mug shot [of Hombre] and the map [of the institution], Herzog distinguishes between a particular type of photographic image as restrictive, normative, and a form of control, as opposed to a flow of cinematic images that emphasize their own immediacy, singularity, and physicality. In other words, the filmmaker distinguishes between an image where meaning is imposed from outside the image (the discursive sphere of the law,

---

[67]Wolfgang Ruf, "Land des Schweigens und der Dunkelheit," *Deutsche Kinemathek*, Sig. 55146, cited in English in Eric Ames, *Ferocious Reality: Documentary According to Werner Herzog* (Minneapolis, MN: University of Minnesota Press, 2012), p. 31. (I have been unable to confirm this citation or to find the original German.)

of medicine, of social structures) and the potential for experiencing the world in the spontaneous interaction with the image itself.[68]

This contrast, developed visually, between coercive confinement, often presented in images of repetition (circling trucks without drivers, dancing chickens, circling chair lifts) as well as images of direct coercion (the interrogations and beatings in *Stroszek* [1977]) and an open flow of nature is a master conceit throughout Herzog's work, as his films scrutinize the possibility of physically significant human action and meaning in relation to that open flow, a possibility typically available only intermittently, perhaps in a ski jump or the transports of ecstatic, rhythmic speech, or perhaps in a moment of vision as if of the whole.

Herzog's films succeed most spectacularly when the attention of the viewer is modulated expertly among moments of absorption in either nature or significant natural-physical action and moments of breakdown, where these modulations develop a plot of either spectacular failure (*Even Dwarfs Started Small, Aguirre, Grizzly Man*) or markedly temporary, but good-enough, redemptive engagement (*The Great Ecstasy of the Woodcarver Steiner, The Dark Glow of the Mountains, The White Diamond, Encounters at the End of the World*) or something mysteriously in-between (*Land of Silence and Darkness, Kaspar Hauser, Stroszek, Little Dieter Needs to Fly, My Best Fiend, Bells from the Deep*). In each case, the modulation of attention, established by the editing, between absorbing ecstatic opticalities and interruptive, reflection-inducing commentary and images of failure, is crucial to the film's success, as is the fit between the modulated attention and the specific plot and theme of the individual film. Herzog himself notes

---

[68]Stefanie Harris, "Moving Stills: Herzog and Photography," in *A Companion to Werner Herzog*, ed. Prager (Oxford: Wiley-Blackwell, 2012), pp. 127–48, at pp. 127–8.

the importance of rhythms of attention in his films in commenting on *Aguirre*, arguably his greatest masterpiece.

> There is an inner flow to most of my films, one that can't be followed with just a wristwatch. In *Aguirre* things steadily move into delirium and become hallucinatory, as if the audience is being taken directly into the interior of things. … There is an image in *Aguirre* that comes immediately after the opening sequence, a minute-long shot of the raging waters of Rio Urubamba, below Machu Picchu. The waters are so violent, almost boiling with rage, completely out of proportion to what a human being might be able to withstand, but a minute of it prepares the audience for an approaching fever dream in the jungle. A filmmaker carefully sows, then harvests. After having seen this image, we are better prepared to accept the disproportion to come, the outrageousness of Aguirre, his grandiose failure to conquer an entire continent with thirty starving and ill-equipped soldiers. These frozen moments

Figure 3 *"The rapids of the Rio Urubamba" from* Aguirre, the Wrath of God *(1972).*

don't necessarily have any significance for the story per se; they connect more deeply, to the film's inner narrative. Aguirre almost holds its breath as the multiple threads of a story moving in all directions are tied in a knot for one brief moment. (Cronin, 94, 95)

A film works best when those moments of held breath fit within, support, and develop the inner logic of the film—its arc of narrative and modulated visual attention—so that the viewer's conviction in what is unfolded visually is maintained from moment to moment. Success does not imply straightforward action-continuity editing. As William van Wert notes, Herzog's films frequently depart from continuity editing in favor of looser, more associative connections, as in cuts in *Land of Silence and Darkness* from a jumping ski-flier, to Fini Staubinger jumping as she says "I always jump when I'm touched," to the deaf-blind touching animals at a zoo, then touching airplane wings, to hand spelling.[69] Instead of developing a single plot, this associative technique enables Herzog to scrutinize and compare multiple marked moments of engagement, grace, communication, and absorption, contrasted with moments of rupture, isolation, and breakdown.

In holding together the developing arc of a film that significantly employs such an associative logic—most prominent in the most experimental documentaries, such as *Fata Morgana* and *Lessons of Darkness*—music is crucial. In particular, music is able to heighten the absorptive-redemptive character of certain moments, presented in images, and Herzog frequently chooses sacred music (Russian Orthodox chants, Arvo Pärt's Stabat *Mater*, Bach's *Jesu bleibt meine Freude*, Gounod's *Ave Maria*) or music that otherwise has a pronounced liturgical and

---

[69]William Van Wert, "Last Words: Observations on a New Language," in *The Films of Werner Herzog*, ed. Corrigan, pp. 51–71.

repetitive feel (the Prelude of Wagner's *Das Rheingold,* Florian Fricke's minimalist compositions, Ernst Reisjeger's solo cello variations) in order to emphasize this character. The music is essential to the unity and effect of the film as a whole. As Herzog puts it, "on practically my first film I came to understand that sound decides the outcome of many battles, that the texture and subtleties of a film often come from its soundtrack. ... The point is that there is no such thing as background music in my films. It's always an integral part of the whole" (Cronin, 303, 67). Herzog is explicit that this use of music both transforms our reception of the images and works to unify the associative logic of the editing.

> Some images become clearer and more understandable when a particular piece of music is playing behind them. They don't physically change, but their inner qualities are exposed and new perspectives opened up. Music is able to make visible what is latent; it reveals new things to us, helps shift our perception and enables us to see deeper into things. We perceive what we would otherwise be oblivious to. An image might not be logical in a narrative sense, but when music is added—even if it somehow disrupts and undermines that image—certain qualities might all of a sudden become transparent that were previously unknown. (Cronin, 67)

Herzog emphasizes the ability of Florian Fricke's music in particular to transform what we see by setting up an aura of the sacred.

> Florian never failed to create music that has forever given us entrée into otherwise inaccessible dimensions. ... Florian's compositions add dimensions to a film that we never knew existed and enable us to shift our perceptions; they make visible what would otherwise remain mysterious and forever hidden in my films, and also what lies buried in our souls. Although when seen alongside Florian's music an image remains the same projection of light, it is somehow

transformed, like the cliff faces and peaks of *The Dark Glow of the Mountains*, which appear to possess a sacred aura and cast a strange spell when we look at them while listening to music by Popol Vuh, Florian's one-man band. (Cronin, 302–3)

The point, for Herzog, of setting up an aura of the sacred in certain images, as well as of modulating attention into and out of such moments across the course of a film, is nothing less than the achievement so far as possible of genuinely human life as such. As the philosopher Ted Cohen once wrote, "being human requires knowing what it is to be human."[70] As occurring in a book on metaphor, this is surely itself a metaphor, the understanding of which will require imaginative investment, rather than a literal falsehood. What it suggests is that our lives are threatened by cliché, inattentiveness, and general failure effectively to use the powers of language, reflection, and conscious agency that are distinctive of human beings. All too often, as Wordsworth puts in his Preface to the Second Edition of *Lyrical Ballads*, our lives are characterized by "a degrading thirst after outrageous stimulation,"[71] insofar as we live under the routinizing pressures of industrial-commercial life and respond to those pressures by seeking escape in distracting spectacles.

Paul Cronin characterizes Herzog's filmic project in just these Wordsworthian Romantic-Modernist terms. (Romantics and Modernists share a sense of the threats to the human posed by industrial-commercial life; while Modernists are perhaps less confident either that the pastoral will save us or that many are apt to resonate to a sense of the problem, Romantics, too, have their shares

---

[70]Ted Cohen, *Thinking of Others: On the Talent for Metaphor* (Princeton, NJ: Princeton University Press, 2008), p. 85.

[71]Wordsworth, "Preface to the Second Edition of *Lyrical Ballads*," in Wordsworth, *Selected Poems and Prefaces*, ed. Stillinger (Boston: Houghton Mifflin Company, 1965), p. 449.

of internal doubts and court moments of circumscribed, temporalized significance rather than doctrinal solutions.[72])

We are, all of us, in this day and age, at the mercy of overwhelming and impersonal historical, economic, and environmental forces, so it's unlikely that the tide of stagnant cinema [that caters to these forces] will ever be beaten back. There are, fortunately, some willing to confront the corrupted, debased, stale, adulterated, ready-made, and cliché-ridden images that surround us. The actions of an enlightened individual or vanguard few, ready to kick back no matter what the odds, those striving for the ideal, can inspire regeneration.[73]

Brigitte Peucker, citing Philip Rosen's criticism of Bazinian realism and applying it to Herzog, characterizes his project similarly, but suggests that it is vain and misbegotten.

The Bazinian project, Rosen convincingly argues, lays bare the "irrationality at the heart of cinema, a desire for *permanence* (of subjective existence, of identity)." Similarly, Herzog's projection of an authorial persona into textuality—through physical investment in the image, through identification with the films' characters, and by a variety of formal means—may likewise originate in a drive for preservation, imaginary as such a solution to the problem of temporality may be.[74]

---

[72]On Romanticism and Modernism thus compared, see Richard Eldridge, *The Persistence of Romanticism* (Cambridge: Cambridge University Press, 2001), pp. 1–30; Eldridge, *Literature, Life, and Modernity* (New York: Columbia University Press, 2008), pp. 1–26, 69–85.

[73]Paul Cronin, "Visionary Vehemence: Ten Thoughts about Werner Herzog," in *Werner Herzog—A Guide for the Perplexed*, ed. Cronin, pp. xi–xli, at p. xxviii.

[74]Brigitte Peucker, "Herzog and Auteurism," in *A Companion to Werner Herzog*, ed. Prager (Oxford: Wiley-Blackwell, 2012), pp. 35–57, at p. 41, citing Philip Rosen, *Change Mummified: Cinema, Historicity, Theory* (Minneapolis, MN: University of Minnesota Press, 2001), p. 34.

Here, however, one may well wonder in reply whether the problem of achieving genuine subjective existence and identity, within the orbit of an unmasterable temporality and in the face of the pressures of industrial-commercial life, is quite so egoistically fantastic as Peucker suggests and whether a response to it via the construction of filmic images is quite so empty. Seeing as something we do actively, via mobilizing our imaginative and emotional attentiveness, is not defined only by the object of attention, and, contra Peucker and some varieties of contemporary criticism, there is more to be hoped for from art than cold, clear-sighted, purely neutral rendering (if that were possible) of the facts of material social reality. Preservation and enhancement of our powers of attention as active subjects can genuinely be in view.

Herzog himself is emphatic that seeing is something we *can* do actively—more actively than we mostly do—by way of engagement with suitable images.

> At the present time, I think that we do not know very much about the process of vision itself. ... This kind of knowledge is precisely what we *need*. We need it very urgently because we live in a society that has *no* adequate images anymore, and, if we do not find adequate images and an adequate language for our civilization with which to express them, we will die out like the dinosaurs. It's as simple as that! We have already recognized that problems like the energy shortage or the overpopulation of the world or the environmental crisis are great dangers for our society and for our kind of civilization, but I think it has not yet been understood widely enough that we also absolutely *need* new images.[75]

---

[75]Herzog, "Images at the Horizon," p. 24. Compare closely parallel remarks in Cronin, pp. 82, 113.

If we cannot *see and feel* imaginatively in attending to natural and sociohistorical reality that there are at least *en mésure* possibilities of meaningful life and experience available to us, then there are few stances left other than cynicism, escapist indulgence, asceticism, and exhausted, depressed reclusion.

Whatever the threats to biological human life and biological life in general that are posed by ecological catastrophes or weapons of mass destruction, the threat to human life with which Herzog is directly concerned is our failure to live fully as actively intelligent and emotionally responsive agents. (Failures so to live count as important potential causes of ecological catastrophes and mass war.) As Romantics and Modernists alike have worried, our lives under modern industrial, commercial, and bureaucratic institutions often enough involve submission to deadening routine, fragmentation into distinct spheres of experience, pronounced social antagonism, and mutual shunning and opacity. By way of the arresting image and the directorial gaze that it embodies, however, we can sometimes be stopped in our tracks and drawn into more animated and attentively interfused thought, imagination, and feeling.

> None of us lead lives of pure logic and order, and similarly, in the best cases, cinema has a strange, mysterious, and illusory quality. It isn't suited to capturing realism and daily life; it has forever been able to reach beyond formal systems of understanding. It sheds light on our fantasies and—like poetry, literature, and music—can illuminate in ways we will never truly be able to grasp. It leads audiences into places where they can observe truth more deeply. I have, with every one of my films, attempted to move beyond facts and illuminate the audience with ecstatic truth. Facts might have normative power, but they don't constitute truth. Facts don't illuminate. Only truth illuminates. By making a clear distinction

between a "fact" and "truth," I penetrate a deeper stratum that most films don't even know exists. The truth inherent in cinema can be discovered only by not being bureaucratically, politically and mathematically correct. (Cronin, 288–9)

The images captured by the camera, itself aimed and focused by the directorial gaze, and thence subjected to editing, function as vehicles through which we might come to think, feel, and imagine more fully and aptly in relation to the phenomena of our natural and social worlds. To undertake to construct images that serve as such vehicles is to explore human nature as such and its possibilities of more fully active life.

Like many people who express themselves through images or writing, I am seeking some insight into human nature. There's nothing exceptional about this; most painters and writers with any skill are working away at the same thing. It isn't that I'm particularly inventive, only that I am able to awaken certain feelings and thoughts inside of you. I can see, on the horizon, unpronounced and unproclaimed images. I can sense the hypnotic qualities of things that to everyone else look unobtrusive, then excavate and articulate these collective dreams with some clarity.

… The images in my films are your images, too. Somehow, deep in your subconscious, you find them, dormant, lurking, like sleeping friends; they correspond with the inner landscapes inside us all and strike directly into the soul of man. Occasionally— perhaps only a dozen times throughout my life—I have read a text, listened to a piece of music, watched a film or studied a painting and felt that my existence has been illuminated. Even if centuries are being bridged, I instantly feel I'm not so alone in the universe. Watching one of my films is like receiving a letter announcing you have a long-lost brother, that your own flesh and blood is out there in a form you had never previously experienced. This is one reason why so many people around the world seem to connect with my films. None of my work is subject to trends or historical movements. (Cronin, 74)

As in Wordsworth, the object and accomplishment are "that the understanding must necessarily be in some degree enlightened, [the] affections strengthened and purified."[76] We live in fuller actualization of our distinctively human powers jointly and by means of artistic attentiveness, not detachedly and from the standpoint of theory alone.

It can strike one as a kind of miracle—perhaps it is a kind of miracle, in being an achievement that is not fully determined by rules and that varies unpredictably across contexts of responsiveness—that heightened imaginative, reflective, and emotional attentiveness can ever be achieved by means of art, in ways that are significant for life. Who knows in advance of the efforts of art and the active responses that those efforts solicit and reward what, if anything, will serve? But the miracle is that sometimes some things do. Herzog testifies to the occurrence of this miracle in his experiences of art, and he announces the pursuit of this miracle as the aim of his filmic work.

Every once in a while it continues to happen to me that when I hear music or see a film just as part of an audience and nothing else, as part of that audience, it suddenly occurs to me that I am not entirely alone anymore, and that's *exactly* what I try to accomplish with my films. Wherever my films are shown, whatever the size of the audience, if I see people coming out of the screening who give me the feeling that they also have not been alone—that they have had the feeling that they are not entirely alone anymore—

---

[76] Wordsworth, "Preface to the Second Edition of *Lyrical Ballads*," p. 448.

then I have done *everything* that I have set out to do! That's *exactly* what I want to do, but much of the time I feel out of tune with most of the industry, with almost everything that's going on—yet, even so, there are *still* enough good people around to make me feel confident.[77]

Which of Herzog's films achieve this miracle of art, by means of which images in which narrative contexts, is the proper subject of critical analysis and judgment, themselves to be tested against the experiences of viewers—against *our* experiences, as we work our ways through individual films, testing verbal formulation and experience of the film against each other, as we undertake to track alertly which animations of the human in its complex embeddedness in nature and culture these films afford.

---

[77]Herzog, "Images at the Horizon," p. 43.

2

Nature

*I believe the common denominator of the universe is
not harmony, but chaos, hostility, and murder.*
—WERNER HERZOG, *GRIZZLY MAN*

As a result of the rise of modern science, with its rejection of final causes and its focus on material particles moving in accordance with physical laws, it is all but impossible not to feel some sense of the absence of providence. No master plan for the embodiment of meaning strikes us as evidently unfolding itself throughout nature and human history. Biological species, if they exist at all as real entities over and above individuals, are nothing more than collocations of self-reproducing organized sets of chemicals that have survived in struggles with other organized sets. Sexuality can seem to be nothing more than a set of biochemically produced impulses that yield reproduction more or less haphazardly, with escape from the pains of life and into pleasure built into the process as nothing more than a naturally selected, overdetermined polyvalent aspect of those impulses. Family life can become an arena of at best accidental and temporary alliances in immediate feeling covering over standing possibilities of opposition, with no one in possession of deep and substantial allegiance to it. Economic and political life tends to become a scene of explicit individual and factional competition for limited material goods rather than a setting for the meaningful cooperative actualization of human powers.

If any sense of active powers of attending, valuing, and willing is retained, as we find ourselves living within a purposeless order of nature, then those powers will typically be taken to be somehow inner and mysteriously protected from the meaningless unfolding of nature.[1] Unsupported by any larger purposes in nature, values that evidently enough differ across distinct human subjects will tend to collapse into functions of simply given preferences, mysteriously resulting from biology plus conditioning. Hence values can come to seem nothing more than things that one happens to have or that happen to one rather than things the objective pursuit of which might give sense and direction to life. Powers of articulating and pursuing values can seem locked within the subject—their active expression in life blocked or at least made problematic by the brute course of nature. There may seem, as Kant puts it in *The Critique of the Power of Judgment*, to be "an incalculable gulf fixed between the domain of the concept of freedom ... and the domain of the concept of nature"[2] wherein we might exercise our powers. How, then, if at all, are we to go on in order to express our active powers and achieve meaningful life, housed, as we seem to be, within an implacably purposeless nature?

Among the host of philosophers who have addressed this question, from Augustine, Descartes, and Kant to Hegel, Heidegger, and Sartre, Nietzsche has the sharpest sense, without illusions, of the sheer

---

[1] See Northrop Frye's useful discussion of an inward turn in modern senses of the self in his "The Drunken Boat," in *Romanticism Reconsidered*, ed. Frye (New York: Columbia University Press, 1963), pp. 1–15. Charles Taylor traces a modern sense of inwardness to Augustine's sense of a power of conversion within confronting a fallen Roman world and a meaningless neo-Stoic nature in Chapter 7, "In Interiore Homine" in his *Sources of the Self* (Cambridge, MA: Harvard University Press, 1992), pp. 143–58.

[2] Immanuel Kant, *The Critique of the Power of Judgment*, trans. Paul Guyer and Eric Matthews (Cambridge, England: Cambridge University Press, 2000), p. 63.

indifference of nature to all purposes, including purposeful human life. In an 1885 notebook entry, he writes:

> This world: a monster of force, without beginning, without end, a fixed, iron quantity of force which grows neither larger nor smaller, which doesn't exhaust but only transforms itself, as a whole unchanging in size, an economy without expenditure and losses, but equally without increase, without income, ... an ocean of forces storming and flooding within themselves, eternally changing, eternally rushing back. ... *This world is the will to power—and nothing besides!*[3]

Adrian del Caro usefully traces Nietzsche's vitalist metaphysics of force in part to his encounters with the 1848 essay "Über Auflösung" [On Discharging] by the German astrophysicist-cosmologist Robert J. Mayer. According to del Caro, Nietzsche

> adopted Mayer's term [*Auflösung*, discharge] for his own uses. Thus ... we find Nietzsche using words such as discharge, ignite, bring to explosion, released, express oneself, explode, react, imitate (*entladen, zünden, zur Explosion bringen, ausgelöst werden, sich auslassen, explodierien, reagieren, nachahmen*) [to describe natural processes, including human actions]. ... From Mayer Nietzsche learned that energy is constantly being stored in organic and inorganic nature, and viewed anthropocentrically, this energy is just waiting to be set off. ... Ultimately, ... Nietzsche takes this idea of discharging into the will to power: everything, everyone is discharging at all times.[4]

[3]Friedrich Nietzsche, *Writings from the Late Notebooks*, ed. Rudiger Bittner, trans. Kate Sturge (Cambridge, England: Cambridge University Press, 2003), §38 pp. 38–9.
[4]Adrian Del Caro, *Grounding the Nietzsche Rhetoric of Earth* (Berlin: de Gruyter, 2004), pp. 325–6.

Nowhere—neither in nature nor in human life within nature—is there the unfolding or even the construction of immanent meaningfulness; force and energy are all.

Once this picture of nature is in place, human efforts at knowing and achieving conditions of meaningful attunement with nature and with one another immediately seem emptily pretentious. Nietzsche draws this conclusion about the emptiness and vanity of intellect and philosophical reflection early in his career in a famous Notebook passage:

> Once upon a time, in some out of the way corner of that universe which is dispersed into numberless twinkling solar systems, there was a star upon which clever beasts invented knowing. That was the most arrogant and mendacious minute of "world history," but nevertheless, it was only a minute. After nature had drawn a few breaths, the star cooled and congealed, and the clever beasts had to die. One might invent such a fable, and yet he still would not have adequately illustrated how miserable, how shadowy and transient, how aimless and arbitrary the human intellect looks within nature. There were eternities during which it did not exist. And when it is all over with the human intellect, nothing will have happened. For this intellect has no additional mission which would lead it beyond human life.[5]

Miserable, shadowy, transient, aimless, arbitrary, and without mission—there is nothing left for intellect to do other than to face up to its condition honestly, without illusions, and to devote itself, at best, to furthering the vitalities and expressions of energy of its individual bearers, locked in forceful competition with one another.

---

[5]Nietzsche, "On Truth and Lies in a Nonmoral Sense" [1873], in *Philosophy and Truth: Selections from the Nietzsche's Early Notebooks of the Early 1970's*, ed. and trans. Daniel Breazeale (Atlantic Highlands, NJ: Humanities Press, 1979), p. 79.

Moral evaluations are subjects for diagnosis through genealogy and psychology that trace their vitalizing functions for those who espouse them divergently within conditions of struggle rather than things to be shared and objectively endorsed. Biologically and socially, "life is itself essentially a process of appropriating, injuring, overpowering the alien and weaker, oppressing, being harsh, imposing your own form, incorporating and at least, at the very least, exploiting."[6]

Positive pictures of what it might be, according to Nietzsche, for at least a few superior beings to discharge their energies affirmatively— if such pictures can even be made consistent with Nietzsche's brutalist naturalism—range from Alexander Nehamas's suggestion that one might, following Nietzsche's account of his life in *Ecce Homo*, at least cultivate a coherent individual style[7] to Gary Shapiro's suggestion of messianic waiting, as we remain caught between fantasies of wholeness and the fact of fragmentation,[8] to Gilles Deleuze's endorsement of ongoing, aggressive nomadism.[9] Without settling questions of interpretive accuracy (or consistency across Nietzsche's *oeuvre*), it is clear that none of these positive pictures endorses or even makes room for general benevolence, cooperation, and shared meaningful life.[10] Nietzsche's vitalist-amoralist metaphysics of nature (including

---

[6]Nietzsche, *Beyond Good and Evil: Prelude to a Philosophy of the Future*, eds Rolf-Peter Horstmann and Judith Norman, trans. Judith Norman (Cambridge: Cambridge University Press, 2002), §259, p. 153.

[7]Alexander Nehamas, *Nietzsche: Life as Literature* (Cambridge, MA: Harvard University Press, 1987).

[8]Gary Shapiro, "How One Becomes What One Is Not," in *Nietzschean Narratives*, ed. Shapiro (Bloomington, IN: Indiana University Press, 1989), pp. 142–67.

[9]Gilles Deleuze, "Nomad Thought," trans. Jacqueline Wallace, in *Semiotexte* III, 1, [*Nietzsche's Return*] (1978), pp. 12–21.

[10]Nehamas's picture admits and endorses these within smaller spheres of intimate friendship, but provides no general social ethics. One might graft standard liberalism onto this picture, contra Nietzsche's metaphysics, but where are the resources for justifying this, if Nietzsche's metaphysics is taken seriously?

human life) as force overwhelms any possibility of a general unfolding or construction of meaning without dramatic structural conflict.

Herzog's sense of the absence of providence in nature is prima facie at least as strong as Nietzsche's. From the relentless swallowing up of the expedition in search of El Dorado by the jungle in *Aguirre* (1972) to the violent maulings by bears and deaths of Timothy Treadwell and Amie Huguenard in *Grizzly Man* (2005), nature is consistently presented as hostile to human powers and interests. As Jennifer K. Ladino remarks, in general, "Herzog's philosophy may be something like 'nature is nasty and so is civilization.'"[11] Commenting on *Fata Morgana* (1970), *Lessons of Darkness* (1992), and *Encounters at the End of the World* (2007), Eric Ames finds "relentless images of a world in ruins, a world of loss, ... [and] an acute awareness of life's transience."[12] Or, as Brad Prager puts it, in Herzog's films in general, nature is "indifferent to our presence, and we, the trespassers, are little more than an interruption in the course of time."[13] The epigraph to *Fitzcarraldo* (1982) informs us that "the forest Indians call this land Cayahuari Yacu, the land in which God was not finished with creation. Only after the disappearance of man, they believe, will God return to finish his work." And the epigraph to *Lessons of Darkness* (1992), attributed to Pascal but in fact written by Herzog, reads "the collapse of the stellar universe will occur—like creation—in grandiose splendor"—in the absence of human beings and in utter indifference to their ever having existed.

---

[11]Jennifer K. Ladino, "For the Love of Nature. Documenting Life, Death, and Animality in *Grizzly Man* and *March of the Penguins*," *ISLE: Interdisciplinary Studies in Literature and Environment* 16, 1 (2009), pp. 53–90, at p. 72.

[12]Eric Ames, *Ferocious Reality: Documentary According to Werner Herzog* (Minneapolis, MN: University of Minnesota Press, 2012), p. 107.

[13]Brad Prager, *The Cinema of Werner Herzog: Aesthetic Ecstasy and Truth* (London: Wallflower Press, 2007), p. 119.

Not only are there the plots, epigraphs, and general themes of the films, Herzog himself has often remarked directly and sharply on the implacable hostility of nature to human purposes and human understanding. In *Burden of Dreams* (1982), the documentary about the making of *Fitzcarraldo* filmed by Les Blank, Herzog insists on the obscenity of human life in nature. When he looks at the jungle, he says, countering Klaus Kinski's perception that it is erotic:

> We have to accept that [nature] is much stronger than we are. Kinski always says that it is full of erotic elements. I don't see it so much [as] erotic. I see it more full of obscenity. It's just ... And nature here is vile and base. I wouldn't see anything erotical here.
>
> I see fornication and asphyxiation and choking and fighting for survival and growing and just rotting away ... Of course, there is a lot of misery but it is the same misery that is all around us. The trees here are in misery, and the birds are in misery. I don't think they sing, they just shriek in pain. Erotic? No! There is an overwhelming fornication! There is a curse on this landscape, and whoever goes too deep into it has a share of this curse! ... We are cursed with what we are doing here! A land where God, if he exists, has created in anger. ... Taking a close look at what's around us, there is some kind of harmony. It is the harmony of overwhelming and collective murder. ... We in comparison ... only sound and look like badly pronounced and half-finished sentences out of a stupid suburban novel, a cheap novel.[14]

Nor is this judgment about the murderous of nature and its hostility to human purposes limited to the Peruvian jungle. In his 1999 *Minnesota Declaration*, Herzog asserts:

---

[14]Les Blank and James Bogan, eds, *Burden of Dreams: Screenplay, Journals, Reviews, Photographs* (Berkeley, CA: North Atlantic Books, 1984), pp. 56–7.

The moon is dull. Mother Nature doesn't call, doesn't speak to you, although a glacier eventually farts. And don't you listen to the Song of Life. We ought to be grateful that the Universe out there knows no smile. Life in the oceans must be sheer hell. A vast, merciless hell of permanent and immediate danger. So much of a hell that during evolution some species—including man—crawled, fled onto some small continents of solid land, where the Lessons of Darkness continue. (Cronin, 477)

Thoughts of this kind are prominent as well in the films themselves. In *Grizzly Man* (2005), Herzog is far from sentimental and far from finding any meaning in nature's role in Treadwell's and Huguenard's deaths: "In all the faces of all the bears that Treadwell ever filmed, I discover no kinship, no understanding, no mercy. I see only the overwhelming indifference of nature. To me, there is no such thing as a secret world of the bears. And this blank stare speaks only of a half-bored interest in food." The written scenario for *Aguirre* reads "the jungle lies in horrible silence, maliciously still, the woodland waiting,"[15] thus casting the jungle as a kind of agent in its malicious waiting—a thought that is displayed implacably in the development of the film. *Fata Morgana* (1970), *Where the Green Ants Dream* (1984), and *Lessons of Darkness* (1992) feature extended shots of abandoned equipment—rusting construction vehicles, assorted airplane parts, and smoking oil derricks—being overcome by natural processes of entropy and decay, processes that likewise will overwhelm the lives and works of human beings in general. *Even Dwarfs Started Small* (1970) shows a driverless van running in endless circles. *Aguirre* (1972) and *Stroszek* (1976)

---

[15]Herzog, *Scenarios*, trans. Martje Herzog and Alan Greenberg (Minneapolis, MN: University of Minnesota Press, 2017), p. 35.

famously end with shots of their protagonists moving in circles: the mad Aguirre revolving in the middle of the Amazon in a God's eye 360-degree tracking shot, and the suicide Stroszek on an otherwise deserted chairlift. All these shots suggest that the works and lives of human beings are desecrations that nature will with time overcome in its self-development that eventually will exclude us. *Encounters at the End of the World* (2007) includes a sustained long shot of a deranged penguin walking away from the ocean and his kind and "heading toward certain death," as well as a shrine in an ice tunnel, composed of a frozen sturgeon and greeting card flowers mounted on small sticks, "framed in a garland of frozen popcorn," all "as if we had wanted to leave one remnant of our presence on this planet … beneath the mathematically precise true South Pole."

Yet the films are neither hectorings about global warming and the destruction of the environment nor counsels of despair. Instead, they interrogate unusual possibilities of meaning within transitory life by investigating the odd and often excessive things human beings do, often in extreme situations and outside the ambit of modern urban life. How can and do we live within an implacably hostile nature that is moved by incomprehensible forces? How can we live in acknowledgment of both its sheer otherness to us and our own passing place within it? What possibilities of alternating horror at our fate and absorption in moments of sudden beauty and in our own activities are open to us, and how, if at all, might a life be well composed out of such alternations? That such questions are in play is evident in Herzog's voice-over description in *Encounters*—presented over shots from the 1950s *The Lone Ranger* television show, of ants milking lice, and of a drawing of a chimp on a goat—of the questions about nature, different from those of a pure nature documentarian, that he used to pitch his filming at McMurdo Station in Antarctica to the National Science Foundation.

My questions about nature, I let them know, were different. I told them I kept wondering why is it that human beings put on masks or feathers to conceal their identity, and why do they saddle horses and feel the urge to chase the bad guy? And why is it that certain species of ants keep flocks of plant lice as slaves to milk them for droplets of sugar? I asked them why is it that a sophisticated animal like a chimp does not utilize inferior creatures? He could straddle a goat and ride off into the sunset.

Like the chimp, we could do many things in the face of our natural situation. We could live and act more or less instinctively, as the ants presumably do, or we could act in a bizarre and apparently purposeless way, as the imagined chimp does. But instead we act in ways that creatively express our nature within nature. We put on masks, identify and chase bad guys, and domesticate animals, in ways that are neither bound entirely by instinct nor obviously bizarre and free from nature, but rather somehow in between instinct and sheer oddness. It is not that we either do or are to do nothing, or that there are no better and worse choices to be made within our situation in nature, in order to acknowledge it, and in order to live with ourselves as fully as we can in doing so. As Herzog remarks in a 2008 interview, in response to a question from Roger Ebert about *Encounters at the End of the World*:

> I made some other films with an apocalyptic note, *Lessons of Darkness* most notably, and *Fata Morgana*. However, I do not think that the end is imminent, but one thing is clear: we are only fugitive guests on our planet. Martin Luther, the reformer, was asked: 'What would you do, if the world came to an end tomorrow?' and he replied, 'I would plant an apple tree.' I would start shooting a new film.[16]

---

[16]Werner Herzog (1979), "Images at the Horizon," in *Herzog by Ebert*, ed. Roger Ebert (Chicago: University of Chicago Press, 2017), pp. 126–7.

Hence at least for Herzog there is at least a possibility of modest, significant action in the framework of our natural human life within a hostile nature—making a film— and there is at least an issue in general for anyone about doing something more rather than less worthwhile in this situation. Or as Herzog memorably puts it in "Twenty-Four Pieces of Advice" listed on the back cover of his collection of interviews with Paul Cronin:

> Always take the initiative. There is nothing wrong with spending a night in jail if it means getting the shot you need. Send out all your dogs and one might return with prey. Never wallow in your troubles; despair must be kept private and brief. Learn to live with your mistakes. Expand your knowledge and understanding of music and literature, old and modern. That roll of unexposed celluloid you have in your hand might be the last in existence, so do something impressive with it. There is never an excuse not to finish a film. Carry bolt cutters everywhere. Thwart institutional cowardice. Ask for forgiveness, not permission. Take your fate into your own hands. Learn to read the inner essence of a landscape. Ignite the fire within and explore unknown territory. Walk straight ahead, never detour. Manoeuvre and mislead, but always deliver. Don't be fearful of rejection. Develop your own voice. Day one is the point of no return. A badge of honor is to fail a film theory class. Chance is the lifeblood of cinema. Guerrilla tactics are best. Take revenge if need be. Get used to the bear behind you. (Cronin, back cover)

While many of these pieces of advice distinctly concern filmmaking, not all of them do, and even the ones that do can be read as self-conscious metaphors for possibilities of significant action in other domains as well.

The films themselves are frequently driven by a sense of an encounter with possibilities of meaning that are afforded by exorbitant images of temporally unfolding natural processes, despite the hostility of nature: the blowing sands of the Sahara in *Fata Morgana* (1970), the rapids rushing straight toward the camera in *Aguirre* (1972), the falling cataracts in *Heart of Glass* (1976) and *The White Diamond* (2004), the flowing fog in *Nosferatu* (1978), the jungle suddenly revealing and then swallowing new threads of the caravan in *Aguirre*, the heat waves shimmering over the salt flats in *Salt and Fire* (2017), the water circulating through the underwater caverns and ice chimneys of *Encounters at the End of the World* (2007). In each case, the camera lingers in full and exact focus on something in motion throughout the screen. As a result, we do not know where within the screen to direct our gaze. There is no particular center of the shot or object on which to focus. We linger with and in the diffused but exact attentiveness of the camera, in an absorption in looking that is a primary mark of the beautiful, while also being aware of the camera's placement by someone and of its taking in something that both calls for and defeats our comprehension—a primary mark of the sublime. In Alan Singer's formulation, Herzog's "mise-en-scène presents the spectacle of a sumptuously particularized reality that, by its very exorbitance, seems to elude conceptualization and so to deny knowledge of its origins."[17] Or, as Laurie Ruth Johnson puts it, in Herzog's signature images "there [is] something that exceeds our grasp, exceeds the boundaries of the frames that restrict our vision, and that was prior to human activities and human 'states,'"[18] as in, for example, our experience of

---

[17]Alan Singer, "Comprehending Appearances: Werner Herzog's Ironic Sublime," in *The Films of Werner* Herzog, ed. Corrigan (London: Routledge, 1986), pp. 183–205, at p. 185.

[18]Laurie Ruth Johnson, *Forgotten Dreams: Revisiting Romanticism in the Cinema of Werner Herzog* (Rochester, NY: Camden House, 2016), p. 147.

a substantial waterfall itself. In the places and processes on which the camera lingers, power in nature that invites and sustains both absorption and a simultaneous sense of one's own frustrated powers of reflection is made manifest.

Herzog observes that his films often begin with engagement with a particular place.

> The starting point for many of my films is a landscape, whether it be a real place or an imaginary or hallucinatory one from a dream, and when I write a script I often describe landscapes that I have never seen, I know that somewhere they do exist and I have *never* failed to find them. Actually, maybe I should say that the landscapes are not so much the impetus for a film, rather they become the film's soul, and sometimes the characters and the story come afterwards, always very naturally. (Cronin, 83)

These landscapes have a soul for Herzog not as a physical component or part of them, but rather insofar as they are numinous sites of unfolding power to which we might somehow resonate: strikingly marked spots of nature as Spinozist *natura naturans* or self-causing activity that both embraces and affects us, as opposed to inert, passive nature as *natura naturata*. What Eric Ames aptly observes about the sites of pilgrimage in the films that treat religious practices applies equally to Herzog's landscapes and scenes of nature's power. "What all these places have in common is the belief that each represents a junction of the material and the immaterial, the exterior and the interior, the visible and the invisible."[19] In *Encounters at the End of the World* (2007), the research physicist Peter Gorham, who is launching high-altitude balloons in order to measure neutrinos, tells us that:

---

[19]Ames, *Ferocious Reality*, p. 74.

Even though I understand it mathematically, and I understand it intellectually, it still hits me in the gut that there is something here around, surrounding me, almost like some kind of spirit or god that I can't touch, and—but I can measure it. I can make a measurement. It's like measuring the spirit world or something like that. You can go out and touch these things.

Junctures of the visible and the invisible then afford us in perception a sense that we might somehow live in nature in more active exercise of our powers, at least temporarily and in perception (as in Kant on natural beauty as what absorbs us in free intuition). "What I'm looking for," Herzog remarks,

is an unspoilt, humane spot for man to exist, an area worthy of human beings where a dignified life can be led, something alluded to in my films. … For Ingmar Bergman, the starting point of a film seems to be the human face, usually that of a woman. For me, it's a physical landscape, whether a real or imaginary or hallucinatory one. (Cronin, 83)

The dignified life that such landscapes might enable and call forth, however fitfully, is a life of the active exercise of powers of attention, acknowledgment, and movement through a landscape, as opposed to the routines of urban commercial life.

Herzog's engagements with nature and landscape trace back to his childhood in Sachrang in the Bavarian Alps, less than a mile from the Austrian border. "As a child," he reports:

I had no knowledge of the outside world; we were totally disconnected. On the way to school in the village we had to cross a forest I was convinced was haunted by witches. Even today, when I pass this spot, I still get the feeling there is something eerie about it. Sachrang was such an isolated place at the time that I didn't know what a banana was until I was twelve, and I didn't make my first telephone call until the age of seventeen. A car was an absolute sensation. We would all sprint after it just to look at the thing, and there is still something exciting to me about watching hundreds of vehicles swishing around on a system of interconnected freeways. I have always felt most comfortable in remote mountains, and part of me has never really adjusted to modern technology; I jump whenever the telephone rings. (Cronin, 10)

Given his sense of childhood attachment to Sachrang, disrupted by his move to postwar, ruined Munich at the age of eleven, Herzog's attractions to numinous spots in nature read in part as attempts to re-experience the fugue-like character of absorbed play that is characteristic of early childhood—almost an attempt to reverse a fall out of naturalness and into self-conscious ego-identity. Frank B. Farrell, thinking perhaps of Wordsworth and Proust, among others, argues (following D. W. Winnicott on ego-formation), that:

In literature or art one has access to a transitional or potential space that formed an earlier stage in the process of self-formation. In this early childhood stage one had to accomplish the work of separation and individuation, of determining the boundaries of the self against what is other, of setting oneself in relation to a world of stable objects, of establishing a secure sense of selfhood over against forces that would threaten to blur or dissolve it.[20]

Given the pains of this labor of individuation, absorption in childhood landscape can function as a kind of restoration of a sense of felt meaningfulness, wholeness, and attachment to things.

---

[20]Frank B. Farrell, *Why Does Literature Matter?* (Ithaca, NY: Cornell University Press, 2004), p. 12.

Here absorption in landscape resembles absorption in the physical activities of sports, wherein one is partially freed from wider issues of responsibility and senses of scrutiny by others. (Herzog has often spoken of his intense physical involvements in playing football and of the effects of this play on his sense of space [Cronin, 114–15, 333–5].) His later childhood in Munich, though without the landscape of the Alps, seems to have been marked by a continuing sense of freedom in movement and absence of scrutiny by others, as "we children took over whole bombed-out blocks and discovered the most amazing things in cellars strewn with rubble. ... With no fathers to listen to and no rules to follow, it was anarchy in the best sense of the word. We invented everything from scratch" (Cronin, 11).

Making a film is then for Herzog part of an effort to recover and to make available to himself and others as grownups a sense of wholehearted involvement in life activity in response to the promptings of extraordinary natural places. In *Self-Portrait* (1986), Herzog presents himself, dramatically attired in a cape, striding through the Bavarian Alps of his childhood, then pausing to write, seated in a notebook, as his voice-over narration announces, "these mountains are the landscape of my childhood. ... I always come back here. It's while walking that I always have the most intensive moments of imagination and of making plans. Then I write a lot and work on projects and screenplays."

If the films are often initiated by an experience of landscape, Herzog is also careful not to suggest that salvific experience is fully available, either for himself or for others, via absorption in *natura naturans*. First, the plots often involve defeat or collapse of human enterprises, as in *Signs of Life* (1968), *Aguirre* (1972), *Heart of Glass* (1976), *Fitzcarraldo* (1982), and *Lessons of Darkness* (1992), or a sense of contact with numinous powers not fully made, but present only in fleeing instants that are impossible to capture, perhaps even impossible to trust, as in *Bells from the Deep* (1993), *Death for Five Voices* (1995), and *The White Diamond* (2004). Second, Herzog is consistently careful to foreground the artifactuality of the image, either through choices of unusual, humanly artifactual subjects of shots (museum vitrines, dancing chickens, caches of stored goods) or through filling the field of vision of the camera with overall motion (rushing rapids, flowing fog) in consistent focus of a kind the human eye cannot manage, so that we are aware that an instrument of recording is being used between us and what is depicted.

Yet—modulated with images of the artifactual and the unusual, and constructed through optical devices—the striking images of nature (cataracts, fog, mist, sand) also often present a sense of nature interacting with itself, in a kind of suspended play of power posed against power in a strange communicative reciprocity. (Wordsworth: "The sounding cataract/Haunted me like a passion: the tall rock, The mountain, and the deep and gloomy wood …. The immeasurable height/Of woods decaying, never to be decayed,/The stationary blasts of waterfalls,/And in the narrow rent at every turn/Winds thwarting winds, bewildered and forlorn,/The torrents shooting from the clear blue sky,/The rocks that muttered close upon our ears,/Black drizzling crags that spake by the way-side/As if a voice were in them, the sick sight/And giddy prospect of the raving stream,/The unfettered clouds and region of the Heavens,/Tumult and peace, the darkness and the light."[21]) In *Of Walking in Ice*, his memoir of his three-week walk from Munich to Paris in November 1974, undertaken as a prophylactic charm to ward off the death of the ailing film scholar Lotte Eisner,

---

[21]Wordsworth, "Lines Composed a Few Miles above Tintern Abbey," in *Selected Poems and Prefaces*, ed. Jack Stillinger (Boston: Houghton-Mifflin, 1965 ll. 75–77), pp. 108–11, at p. 109; *Prelude*, Book VI, "Cambridge and the Alps," in *Selected Poems and Preface*, (Boston: Houghton-Mifflin, 1965 ll. 624–35), p. 269.

Herzog produces verbal equivalents that echo Wordsworth of his filmic images of nature acting upon nature. "Apples lie rotting in the wet clay soil around the trees, nobody's harvesting them. On one of the trees, which seemed from afar like the only tree left with any leaves, apples hang in mysterious clusters close to one another. There isn't a single leaf on the wet tree, just wet apples refusing to fall."[22] The apples do not simply rot, but agentively *lie rotting* into the surrounding soil; the apples hang *close to one another* as if in silent awareness of their mutual presences, and they are in a continuous present agentively *refusing to fall*. Similarly:

> The fir trays sway against each other, crows are rushing against the strong wind, making no headway. Upon long stalks of rye a whole community has been built, on each stalk a house. The houses waver majestically atop their stalks, the entire community swinging and swaying. The hawk sustains itself against the wind above the fir trees, remaining in one spot, then it is borne aloft and changes its course.

"Against," "against," "sustains itself," "remaining"—power communicating reciprocally with power, in a kind of self-perpetuating, active stasis; the tops of the stalks of rye forming a community of habitation, swinging and swaying. Nature is here a more continuously unfolding, all but animate mysterious process than a mere complex set of particles in space.

Despite, however, the sense, available in perception, of unfolding, absorbing presence in scenes of natural power suspended against natural power, no plot of nature's development becomes evident. These scenes of natural power remain indecipherable—an aspect of Herzog's sense of the priority of the image and perception over the word and *logos*—and

---

[22]Herzog, *Of Walking in Ice*, trans. Martje Herzog and Alan Greenberg (Minneapolis, MN: University of Minnesota Press, 2015), p. 87.

no continuously fulfilling natural home for human life and activity is disclosed. Spinoza argued that we could adjust ourselves to the unfolding active power of nature as *natura naturans* through appropriate intellectual contemplation, so that we might achieve something like Stoic *ataraxia* or calmness of mind. Hegel rejected Spinoza's neo-Stoic contemplativism in favor of a picture of appropriate familial, economic, and political activity housed within a good-enough nature, through which we might achieve freedom as being-with-oneself-in-another, *bei sich selbst in einem anderen*, thence arriving at stability and self-assurance in activities and relationships. Herzog's picture, in contrast, is both more plausible and bleaker. "In ... Herzog's films," as Peter W. Jansen aptly puts it,

> Landscapes exist as a feverish dream (*The Mystery of Kaspar Hauser*), an obsession (*Signs of Life*), and in the minds of people (*Land of Silence and Darkness*). Above all, [nature] passes by them, above them, without taking notice of their presence or leaving its mark on them, devoid of people, appealing directly to the viewer's emotions, consciousness, memory, and frame of mind. ... The cinema of subjectivity offers itself as a poetic-mystical refuge for the self, that sees itself as torn from the *unio mystica* with nature and irreparably wounded since its rude awakening at birth. The image of the landscape becomes a vague and unsettled distant memory of a lost primal state, in which idyll and might, the individual and the world, the self and the other are still facets of one and the same sensation, and neither moral nor political categories.[23]

---

[23]Peter W. Jansen, "innen/außen/innen: Funktionen von Raum und Landschaft [bei Herzog, Kluge, Straub]," in *Herzog/Kluge/Straub*, eds Peter W. Jansen and Wolfram Schütte (München: Hanser, 1979), pp. 69–112, at p. 69; cited in English translation in Gertrud Koch, "Blindness as Insight: *Land of Silence and Darkness*," in *The Films of Werner Herzog*, ed. Corrigan, pp. 73–86, at p. 83.

Jansen's formulation "neither moral nor political categories" implies correctly that Herzog presents nature and landscapes as something other than sites of political and social habitation. Instead, Herzog offers at best what Beatrice Hanssen (commenting on Friedrich Hölderlin) calls "a philosophical *anamnesis* of nature … a reflection to the second power in which reflection ponder[s] its own negativity and finitude."[24] That is, the experience of Herzog's images of nature includes an experience on the part of the viewer of being left outside the movement of nature, as nature relates itself to itself in moments of poised suspension and discloses itself to the camera as a recording instrument that includes natural processes. This sense of outsiderliness to nature's active processes is further reinforced by our awareness of the constructed character of the image (despite the camera's registering of and participation in natural processes). This awareness is marked and sustained by the fullness of focus of Herzog's shots across the large-screen image, since this comprehensive focus is something the human eye can neither match nor take in all at once, so that we are in part left out of what the camera is doing in its registerings. And it is marked and sustained by the typical extended length of Herzog's shots, a length that far exceeds the purposes of mere discursive recognition of what one is seeing, so that one is forced into awareness of one's own activity of imperfect looking. Reinhold Steingröver suggests that Herzog's sense of human outsiderliness to nature is informed in part by Heinrich von Kleist,[25] a writer about whom Herzog remarked that "sometimes—even if centuries are

---

[24]Beatrice Hanssen, "'Dichtermut' and 'Blödigkeit': Two Poems by Friedrich Hölderlin Interpreted by Walter Benjamin," in *Walter Benjamin and Romanticism*, eds Beatrice Hanssen and Andrew Benjamin (New York: Continuum, 2002), pp. 139–62, at pp. 141–2.

[25]Reinhold Steingröver, "Encountering Werner Herzog at the End of the World," in *A Companion to Werner Herzog*, ed. Prager (Oxford: Wiley-Blackwell, 2012), pp. 466–84, at pp. 471–2.

being bridged—you find a brother and instantly know you are no longer alone."[26] In Kleist's "The Fable without a Moral," an isolated protagonist laments the fact that the horse standing before him with bit and saddle has been taught "arts" of which he "knows nothing" so that he is unable to ride the horse naturally in something like naked merger with its unfolding natural powers in running, but instead must ride it, if at all, on a track and making use of human contrivances. Just so, Steingröver argues, "the paradox Herzog encounters while filming at Antarctica [for *Encounters at the End of the World*, 2007] is a familiar one for his oeuvre ... : the search for images of humanity's unmediated encounters with nature must fail because the moment of encounter coincides with the moment of spoiling the formerly unseen landscape."[27] At least for us—we beings who have fallen into self-consciousness and reflection by falling via socialization into language and culture—purely immediate, participatory experience in nature is not a genuine possibility. Reflection and the awareness of the possibility of reflection are always part of the structure of experience, at least implicitly, as aspects of reflection's "negativity and finitude."

It is no surprise, then, that Herzog frequently describes himself not as filming nature or landscapes full stop, but rather as filming what he calls inner landscapes or landscapes of the mind.

For me a true landscape is not just a representation of a desert or a forest. It shows an inner state of mind, literally inner landscapes, and it is the human soul that is visible through the landscapes presented in my films, be it the jungle in *Aguirre*, the desert in *Fata Morgana*, or the burning oil fields of Kuwait in *Lessons of Darkness*. This is my real connection to Caspar David Friedrich, a man who

---

[26]Herzog, *Herzog on Herzog*, ed. Paul Cronin (New York: Faber and Faber, 2002), p. 136.
[27]Steingröver, "Encountering Werner Herzog at the End of the World," p. 477.

never wanted to paint landscapes *per se*, but wanted to explore and show inner landscapes.[28]

Thus Herzog describes Mt. Kailash, the site of a Buddhist pilgrimage in the form of a chora or three-day, fifty-two kilometer circumnavigation of its base at 17,000 feet, as the peak looms above at almost 22,000 feet, as "not only a very impressive pyramid of black rock with a cap of ice and snow on its top, it immediately strikes the voyager as something much deeper—an inner landscape, an apparition of something existing only in the soul of man."[29] Here an inner landscape is presented not, as it were, in itself, but rather as an actual landscape experienced as a numinous place in a mixture of emotion, imagination, perception, and reverie, where this numinous place is mysteriously beyond yet also encloses the human.

These inner landscapes as imaged on film draw us toward a sense of living meaningfulness in nature, even if it makes little or no place for us, and Herzog is not at all prepared to accept either a physicalist-materialist picture of nature or an instrumentalist-utilitarian picture of human action. (As Jansen puts it, "idyll and might, the individual and the world, the self and the other" remain "facets of one and the same sensation."[30]) Mind and nature call or speak to one another through these images, without plot, and with possibilities of acknowledgment of fitful individual power as part of nature's power, yet crossed with negativity and finitude. Hence it is both possible and important to discern something in nature to which we might resonate inchoately, if we are to have any hope of avoiding disasters that stem

[28]Herzog, *Herzog on Herzog*, p. 136.

[29]Herzog, "Introduction" in *Pilgrims: Becoming the Path Itself*, ed. Lena Herzog (London: Periplus, 2004), p. 11.

[30]Jansen,"innen/außen/innen," cited in English translation in Koch, "Blindness as Insight," in *The Films of Werner Herzog*, ed. Corrigan, p. 83.

from unchecked egoism and instrumentalism. Herzog wants his work and his images to address our situation productively, albeit without the hubris of thinking that human beings and their interests are somehow the telos of nature's self-development. While avoiding philosophical hubris, we nonetheless can and should do something, or live in a more aptly human way, according to images that afford at least a partial and temporalized sense of power responding to power and hence of fuller life than is available within daily urban routine. Not knowledge of apt courses of life, but instead acknowledgment in feeling and perception of our fundamental situation in nature is what is in view.

Herzog employs a variety of distinct visual strategies in order to construct the images that present inner landscapes as numinous places. Most generally, there is what Thomas Elsaesser calls Herzog's practice "of not conceiving the diegetic action around the point of view shot and its inevitably psychologizing structure of inference. One might say that Herzog's mise-en-scene seeks to create a point of view, without the point of view shot as its basis."[31] Often this avoidance of a particularized psychological point of view is achieved by using a very high shot of an extended landscape, including unfolding natural processes, that is held for an unusually long period of time, or at any rate a period of time that exceeds what would be necessary in order to establish that any particular agent is up to any particular activity within the scene. As Herzog himself puts it in describing the opening of his first feature film, *Signs of Life* (1968), "the opening credits, for example, hold for an unusually long time with a single shot of a mountain valley. It gives you time to really climb deep inside the landscapes, and for them to climb inside you. It shows you that these

---

[31] Thomas Elsaesser, "An Anthropologist's Eye: *Where the Green Ants Dream*," in *The Films of Werner Herzog*, ed. Corrigan (London: Routledge, 1986), pp. 133–56, at p. 154.

are not just literal landscapes you are looking at, but landscapes of the mind too" (Cronin, 39). Crucially, the mind in question is not that of any particular protagonist; no characters have yet even been introduced as these opening credits roll. Instead human mindedness as such, distributed throughout each viewer, is drawn into felt responsiveness to the landscape. For each viewer, one by one, "you … really climb deep inside the landscapes, and [they] climb inside you." As Dana Benelli remarks about the sustained, extreme long-shot openings of both *Signs of Life* (1968) and *Aguirre* (1972), "the world is displayed as vast, natural (ahistorical) and indifferent to humanity. The individual is presented as a minuscule element of this vast whole, ever in danger of being engulfed and lost in the world's vastness."[32]

When motion on the part of a protagonist through such a landscape does occur, it is typically not the teleological movement of a distinct heroic or otherwise exemplary individual moving toward a consciously held, reasonable goal, but instead something repetitive and obsessional, from Stroszek's pointless patrolling of an all but deserted landscape on the Greek island of Kos, finding only a vast field of a thousand rotating windmills (*Signs of Life*, 1968), to Aguirre's doomed, obsessive quest for El Dorado (*Aguirre*, 1972), to Jonathan Harker as a vampire riding off across the desert (*Nosferatu*, 1979), and to the disoriented penguin wandering away from its kind and toward death in *Encounters at the End of the World* (2007). In general, as Benelli puts it in commenting on *Signs of Life*:

> Motion is an elemental life sign; to stop moving is to disappear (to fail to attract and hold attention in the frame). … Circular forms, whether literal or figurative, and the textual "circles"

---

[32]Dana Benelli, "The Cosmos and Its Discontents," in *The Films of Werner Herzog*, ed. Corrigan (London: Routledge, 1986), pp. 89–103, at p. 92.

created by narrative repetition, become associated with themes of meaningless passivity (the boredom of routine in the fort), vitiating containment (the exhausted fly in the toy owl), entrapment (the buried rooster), a world utterly permeated by these sorts of experiences (the strikingly long pan of the valley of windmills), and, ultimately, madness (the windmills again).[33]

Or, in the happier figures—Graham Dorrington in *The White Diamond* (2004), Juliane Koepcke in *Wings of Hope* (1998), Dieter Dengler in *Little Dieter Needs to Fly* (1997)—there is typically a kind of ironic, tragicomic awareness of the more or less itinerant character of one's course of life, of its being hostage to fortune. ("Guerilla tactics are best. … Get used to the bear behind you.")

In general, in both the documentaries and the fiction films, Herzog, as Thomas Elsaesser puts it, frequently "push[es] the discrepancy between the perspective of the protagonists and that of the audience to an extreme,"[34] as we see those protagonists moving obsessively and without any achievable point, without quite knowing what they are doing or why, frequently ending in disaster, sometimes in irony and good luck. Happy marriages, friendships, fulfilling work, and accomplished, reasonable, more or less normal social identities—the sorts of things that might typically be thought to yield meaning in life—are typically absent. The point is to focus not on occupations or social roles that one might take up in order to live in fulfillment, but instead to highlight how tentative, unscripted, and hostage to fortune and natural processes our lives are. As Herzog himself puts it in an early review of American experimental films, but in a characterization that applies equally to his own work, "the visions

---

[33]Ibid., pp. 94, 95.
[34]Elsaesser, "An Anthropologist's Eye," p. 154.

happen of their own; they are not forced from literature or from a script. ... Visionary seeing demands a new relation to reality ... [and] a new style of representation [that involves] the documentary character of every film recording, which is consciously manipulated through camera movement, editing, or laboratory work, in order to overcome an anachronistic naturalism."[35] Here the anachronistic naturalism is the thought that we mostly do or can know what we're doing and achieve fulfillment through modern life as usual in more or less standard industrial, urban, or suburban social settings. The documentary character of any film recording is the ability of the camera when used appropriately to disclose more fundamental truths about the fragility and indigence of human life in nature. Through deeper images of natural processes and inner landscapes—images that reject anachronistic naturalism—we are, to repeat Koepnick's terms, to "experience the world of our perception as something beautifully ambivalent, enigmatic, in flux, inassimilable, and unpredictable."[36] When the attempt to afford this kind of experience works badly, as in *Salt and Fire* (2017), a film that Nick Allen called "fundamentally bad" and "at its best, Herzog's version of camp; at its worst, unwitting self-parody,"[37] with an audience rating score of 15 percent on Rotten Tomatoes, the result can be portentous, empty, and off-putting. But when it works well, as it more frequently does, we have the sense of encountering fundamental conditions of human life in nature, as if for the first time.

---

[35]Herzog, "Rebellen in Amerika: Zu Filmen des New American Cinema," *Filmstudio*, May 1964, pp. 55–60, cited in Ames, *Ferocious Reality*, p. 54.

[36]Lutz Koepnick, "Herzog's Cave: On Cinema's Unclaimed Past and Forgotten Futures," *Germanic Review: Literature, Culture, Theory* 88, 3 (2013), p. 273.

[37]Nick Allen, "Review of *Salt and Fire*," archived at: https://www.rogerebert.com/reviews/salt-and-fire-2017.

Fata Morgana (1971) is the most experimental, improvisatory, and non-narrative of Herzog's films. It has not been widely acclaimed as a success. In his 1971 *New York Times* review, Vincent Canby called it "a doggerel nightmare that tries, too late, to deny the failed poetic aspirations of its earlier sections by employing the methods of the Cinema of the Ridiculous."[38] Yet it expresses Herzog's hallucinatory, bleak, anti-institutional vision of human life in nature especially forcefully, partly in virtue of its significant departure from ordinary narrative conventions. The title is an Italian term, taken from the Arthurian legend of the sorceress Morgen le Fay, for a mirage that appears in a narrow band just above the horizon. Instead of focusing on characters in action, the film is both inspired and dominated by the landscape. Initially, Herzog had planned to shoot a film about science fiction aliens arriving on earth to find only the detritus of a dying planet. But instead of tracking the experiences of identifiable visitors, he produced a nonfiction report on the Sahara and on the oddities of human life there, as though the camera and we the viewers were the aliens seeing the earth as a whole for the first time. In Herzog's later characterization of how the production of the film developed:

> On the first day of shooting I decided to scrap this idea [to shoot a science-fiction film about aliens arriving on Earth]. The visionary aspects of the desert landscape that had taken hold of me were much more powerful than any ideas I had brought with me, so I junked the story, opened my eyes and ears, and filmed the desert mirages. I asked no questions; I just let it happen. My reactions to what I was seeing around me were like those of an eighteen-month old baby exploring the world for the first time. The film is like those moments when you are half asleep in the early morning

---

[38]Vincent Canby, "Sounding the Alarm on the Sahara," *New York Times*, October 8, 1971.

and a series of wild, uncontrollable things flow through your mind. There are rarely orderly thoughts and images, yet they belong to you and have a mysterious coherence to them. It was as if I had woken up after a night of drunkenness and experienced a moment of real clarity. All I had to do was capture what I was seeing and I would have my film. (Cronin, 59–60)

Herzog is then explicit that the film's main concern is the quality of human life in the particular landscape of the Sahara, as though the desert brought out fundamental facts about human life that we otherwise suppress or fail to notice.

Deserts are mysterious places. The Sahara is so unreal it's like being in a perpetual dream or on another planet. It isn't merely a landscape, it's a way of life. The solitude is the most overwhelming thing; a hushed quality envelops everything. At night the stars are so close that you can harvest them with your outstretched hands. Although we were driving, the spirit of our journey was like one made on foot, something only people who have travelled through the desert can truly understand. My time there was part of an ongoing quest. (Cronin, 61)

The opening of *Fata Morgana* consists of eight successive views, shot from a distance across a field, of a single airplane—we are initially unsure whether it is the same plane or a different one each time—descending to land toward the camera. The effect of this opening sequence is a radical defamiliarization and depsychologization, something like the defamiliarizing effect that can be achieved by repeatedly pronouncing a single word out loud: one feels its strangeness and a sense of mystery and wonder that it has a use at all. Just so: this opening sequence primes us to see the earth and human life on it as if for the first time.

The film is divided into three main parts—Creation (39 minutes), Paradise (26 minutes), and The Golden Age (14 minutes)— where the titles reinforce the sense of viewing life anew and from outside participation in it. Part I is accompanied by voice-over narration, as the seventy-two-year-old German film scholar Lotte Eisner, Herzog's friend and inspiration, reads in an authoritative voice a version, written by Herzog, of Popul Vuh, the creation myth of the K'iche' people of the highlands of Guatemala. The text explicitly establishes a God's eye or radically alien point of view. "Invisible was the face of the earth. Only the seas gathered under the firmament. That was all." As the narrative continues, backed by music by Couperin, Mozart, and Handel, static long shots alternate with tracking long shots, juxtaposing images of the empty desert, rusting oil barrels, abandoned airplane parts, mirages with an unidentifiable vehicle moving within them at a great distance, and water. Generally, the tracking shots with the camera in motion are more lyrical, in being suggestive of life and intimacy with the landscape, while the static shots concentrate more on the detritus of civilization. Erica Carter aptly describes the structure of the film as kind of search for life, present both to the camera and within the camera's motion that takes place outside the boundaries of ordinary, human, continuous development from birth to death.

The search for a mobility that extends into infinite space is reinforced on the one hand by the film's countless long tracks, pans, and aerial shots, on the other by a montage that disrupts spatial coherence by connecting sequences from quite different locations: now the Sahara, now the Ivory Coast or East Africa. In a sequence late in Part I, the film cuts from a long track along Saharan sands, to a soaring aerial view, shot in East Africa, of flamingoes dissolving into a blur of pink. As in the earlier sand dune sequence, the organizing logic here is neither that of a narrative, nor of ethnographic spectacle, but of a sustained mobility that confounds realist perception and triggers the experience of a de-spatialized filmic time.[39]

By "de-spatialized filmic time," Carter means that there is no continuity editing or tracking of a continuous action through space on the part of an identifiable protagonist. Instead, the mobile camera seems to be tracking general conditions of life as such in nature, life that is itself interrupted, fragmentary, unfulfilling, and yet mysteriously evocative—as if parceled out to those who receive it in ways that remain unknown and unknowable to them and to us, yet able to hold the gaze of the camera. The first human figure—an isolated child in the desert, shot at a distance—does not appear until twenty-five minutes into the film. The other figures we see later—a child holding a desert fox, a male bordello drummer wearing goggles and singing into a radically distortion-producing microphone, accompanied by a bored female piano player, three giggling Germans reciting nonsense verse, a German lecturing on his interest in the monitor lizard's ability to survive in the desert, a group of children chanting "Blitzkrieg is madness," a second German, wearing a scuba outfit, explaining the anatomy of the sea turtle and then descending into a pool to follow the turtle he has released, among others—are shown out of context, so as to suggest that what they do is somehow both obsessive and an at best intermittent flicker of life. These images of human beings are surrounded by more extended images of the desert, abandoned construction sites, deserted mud flats, and apparently empty settlements. Herzog describes the technique of the film as a matter of capturing what is strange, absurd, and desolate in human life in nature.

---

[39]Erica Carter, "Werner Herzog's African Sublime," in *A Companion to Werner Herzog*, ed. Prager, pp. 329–35, at p. 340.

It was important to understand how to move with the rhythm and sensuousness of the landscape, so I was constantly slowing down and speeding up. All the strange machinery you see in the film, these absurd and desolate fragments of civilisation simmering under the sun, was part of an abandoned Algerian army depot. We would find things lying in the middle of the desert—a cement mixer or something like that—a thousand miles from the nearest major settlement or town. Was it ancient astronauts who placed these things there? Were they man-made? If so, what purpose could they possibly serve? These are the embarrassed landscapes of our planet, the kinds of images that appear throughout my work from *Fata Morgana* to *Lessons of Darkness* and beyond. (Cronin, 64)

The film ends with an extended long shot of a vehicle—possibly the VW van that Herzog and Jörg Schmidt-Reitwein used to film the tracking shots, possibly the all but unidentifiable vehicle seen from a distance in Part I—moving continuously from left to right and slightly away from the viewer, as the camera tracks it, backed by an instrumental portion of "Sea of Joy" by *Blind Faith*—traveling music par excellence—until at last it disappears out of the right edge of the frame. The effect is one of taking departure, from the desert, from the viewer, from the film, and from human life as such, having encountered it in all its fitful strangeness and mystery. This effect, as a dominant mood and achieved through the use of many of the same techniques (long shots, tracking shots, evocative music, unexpected montage) is one that appears regularly throughout Herzog's films, as he continues to track human life in nature. In the best films, this effect appears more closely tethered to a coherent narrative, but it is the combination of these techniques of attention with narrative, rather than either one alone, that is singularly responsible for a sense of extraordinary disclosure.

Aguirre (1972) opens with one of the most famous and compelling
sequences in all of Herzog's oeuvre: backed by haunting, very slowly
modulating, chorale-like organ and vocals without words, an aerial
shot moves down through fog to a mountain trail, where we see a
party of explorers snaking single file across the rocks and through
woods and mist. A second aerial shot again moves through the mist
to find a now longer line of soldiers and bearers, still dwarfed by the
rocks. As the camera pans down, a new bit of the caravan appears in
the extreme lower left foreground, making us aware that the line of
the expedition is far larger than we had imagined. The Indian bearers
become more prominent objects of the camera's attention. There is
a cut to a wooden crate tumbling down the side of the mountain
and shattering. Indians, llamas, and conquistadors move toward the
camera in moderate close-up. Some Indians are in chains, and some
are carrying a sedan chair. Under the titles, further mid-close-ups
show a well-dressed Spanish woman, soldiers in armor, and Indians
carrying wooden crates enclosing chickens and then a heavy wooden
wheel. Barefoot Indians drive small native pigs down the narrow,
rocky track. One Indian carries a small, clothed, wooden Madonna
statuette, followed by a robed monk, barefoot and prominently
wearing a cross. An oddly buckle-backed conquistador leads a young
blond woman by the hand, close toward the camera and then past
it, down the mountainside. A somewhat corpulent man in armor
feels his way along behind them. From behind, we see men in armor
carrying a cannon down the path away from us that the others have
taken. There is a sudden mid-close-up cut to a cannon falling down
the mountainside, exploding as it lands amid dense undergrowth,
followed by a cut to a wider view of the explosion against the jungle
backdrop with a river in the foreground. The film cuts to show mists
moving upward through trees with the sound of the river in the
background, then to the native pigs on the edge of the river amid

rocks, with a few boots on the edge of the shot. Two Spaniards—an intense, bearded man, and the oddly buckled one—fill the frame and gaze down toward the river, with only the sound of the river and no music. The buckled one says, "nobody can get down that river alive," and the bearded one replies, "I say we can do it [*Ich sag dir, es geht doch.*] … Things are looking up [*Und jetzt dann geht es bergauf*]." From somewhat below him and to his left, the buckled man turns to look up at him with skepticism, suspicion, and resentment, and then says, "Now it's downhill [*Jetzt geht es bergab*]." Finally, successive shots of rapids fill the frame, with the camera as an instrument of perfect attention to nature's non-centered surging, as the haunting music returns.

The entire almost six-minute sequence is a perfect synecdoche of civilization as such in nature that the subsequent course of the film will play out. Nature as a scene of active powers surrounds and threatens human life, as the jungle continues in its growth and the river in its surging, no matter what human beings do. Human beings organize their motions through nature in ways that include the domestication of animals, violence (the armor and cannons), and sexual and racial differentiations. Accidents happen (the exploding cannon), and exactly where anyone is going is unclear. Success is unlikely, and optimism is unrealistic ("*Jetzt geht es bergab*").

As a result of this synecdoche, some identification with members of the expedition is established on the part of the viewer, distributed unclearly across various members of the party, no matter who or what they turn out to be, as the fate of humanity seems to be at stake. It is impossible not to wonder, "Will they survive? Will they succeed in their expedition in the face of nature's presences?"

The film then ends with an equally famous, haunting shot of the buckled man, Aguirre, who has usurped control of the smaller exploring party, whose fortunes we have followed, that has been sent

down the river to search for El Dorado as an offshoot of the larger
expedition. On a small, now decrepit raft in the middle of the river
(the Urubamba) that has now opened out into the Amazon within a
surrounding, flat jungle, Aguirre in close-up cradles the head of his
mortally wounded daughter (the blonde young woman), caresses her
hair, and wonders at the blood on his right hand. The raft is overrun
with monkeys, and no one else seems to be alive. In close-up, Aguirre
proclaims to the camera, "when we reach the sea, we'll build a bigger
ship, and sail north to take Trinidad from the Spanish crown." The
monkeys are shown clambering across the useless cannon. From the
rear, showing his shoulders and with his head slightly turned toward
the camera, Aguirre goes on, "Then we'll sail on and take Mexico
away from Cortes." Then, over shots of the monkeys, in voice-over,
"What a great treachery that will be!" As Aguirre walks across the
half-submerged raft amid chattering monkeys and dead bodies stuck
with Indian spears, "Then we shall control all of New Spain and
will produce history as others produce plays." Aguirre sinks to his
knees on the very edge of the raft, amid monkeys, then rises to walk
awkwardly back across the ends of its half-submerged logs, until he
reaches the opposite end, from which monkeys scatter. He crosses to
the cannon, where there are more monkeys and another dead body.
Then he walks under the tattered canopy tent, across the raft. We see
him from the rear as he continues walking, announcing:

> I, the Wrath of God, will marry my own daughter and with her
> I'll found the purest dynasty the earth has ever seen. Together we
> shall rule the whole of this continent. [Picking up one of the small
> monkeys and addressing it at face level, in profile to the camera, as
> the monkey shits on him.] We'll endure. I am the Wrath of God.
> [Turning to full face, with his eyes away from us, up and to the
> right,] Who else is with me?

Figure 4 *"I am the Wrath of God. Who else is with me?" from* Aguirre, the Wrath of God *(1972).*

Aguirre tosses the monkey aside. The camera cuts to the sun high up in the frame (shining on the just and the unjust alike), as the signature organ-choral music returns. There is a cut to a wide shot of the flat, broad surface of the Amazon, with the camera moving over and across it. The raft comes into view as the camera approaches and then circles it, showing it alone in the river, and Aguirre standing alone on it, amid the dead and the monkeys, in a 540-degree pan. There is a fade to black, and the credits roll.

It is an image of perfect madness in the form of an ambition to pure (incestuous procreation with his own daughter), godlike self-creation and assertion of naked will, all defeated by the implacable course of nature. We cannot help but differentiate ourselves from nature and express our wills, whatever violence, injustice, and fury that differentiation entails, especially in the case of European ambitions to the conquests of nature and of native life, and we cannot help but fail in madness as we do so. We are both with Aguirre, European civilization's mad representative, and outside him, in seeing him from the camera's merciless point of view and ability to capture nature as such.

In between these two perfect synecdoches of civilization-in-nature that open and end the film, we have mostly seen how Aguirre's ambition develops ruinously and with casual brutality and disregard for others, and we have seen the continual decay of the organized life of the exploring party as a result of abrupt, unexplained Indian attacks from the edge of the jungle, as though the jungle itself were doing its work. Religion is shown as nothing but a servile prop to violent political authority. The sheer force of Aguirre's will undoes a settled order of rules in ousting and then ordering the murder of Don Pedro de Ursua, appointed by Pizarro as the initial commander of the exploring party, whose wife Inés then hauntingly walks alone into the jungle to die. Ursua's replacement, Don Fernando de Guzmán, whom Aguirre installs as Emperor of El Dorado, with himself continuing as "second-in-command," is fat and interested in little but consuming his excessive share of what food there is. The legal proceedings that occur—the trial of Ursua, the proclamation of Guzmán as emperor—are nothing but shams. Early on, eight men caught in an eddy in the rapids on the opposite side of the river from the main party are shot to death at night, presumably on Aguirre's orders, thwarting Ursua's plan to rescue them. The Indians acting as bearers suffer their enslavement more or less stoically, despite the fact that some of them are educated and of royal lineage. A native village is burned and looted. Aguirre's naked will is all, in forming what vestiges of European civilization there are. And it is not enough. Neither civil order nor human life survives.

La Soufrière (1977), a short documentary about the putatively imminent eruption of a volcano by that name on the island of Saint

Vincent, is more optimistic, guardedly, about a certain form of stoical human life in nature. Like *Aguirre*, the film opens with an aerial shot, here of the smoking volcano, accompanied by Herzog's voice-over narration: "I was immediately fascinated when I read that one single poor peasant had refused to be evacuated" when the order to leave the island was issued. This opening is followed by shots of the deserted town of Basse-Terre, including an abandoned police station—"It was a comfort to us not to have the law hanging around"— deserted streets, traffic lights signaling to no one, with scavenging dogs and donkeys, and a vacant pier, all with the smoking volcano in the background. Echoing *Fata Morgana*, Herzog as narrator observes, "it was as spooky as a science fiction locale" in its buildings and streets empty of human life. After a number of hand-held shots with the camera moving through the streets and then up the volcano to the crater's edge, Herzog presents photographs from the 1901 eruption of a volcano in Martinique that left 30,000 dead and only one survivor. From this, the film cuts to images of the smoking La Soufrière. At last, after lingering on the mountain, the film then finds its proper subjects: three men who had refused to leave. The first and most important is found sleeping under a tree with his cat. "I hated to wake him up." Upon being awakened and asked why he is there, the man, dressed in ragged clothes and evidently indigent, replies:

> I'm here because it's God's will. I'm waiting for death, and I wouldn't know where to go anyway. I haven't a cent. And no one knows when it will come. It is as God has commanded. He will not only take me to his bosom, but everyone else. Like life, death is forever, I haven't the slightest fear. Because it's God's will, and no one can tell when death will come.

After briefly turning to one of the other two remaining on the island, the camera returns to this first man, who adds, "I'm at peace with myself, with what's inside me," whereupon he sings a Creole folk song. Following a short exchange with the third man who's remained, the camera returns to the smoking volcano, holding it in distant shots for 3:25, backed by the most triumphant portion of Siegfried's Funeral March from *Götterdämmerung*, as Herzog concludes the voice-over narration, telling us:

It will always remain a mystery why there was no eruption. Never before in the history of volcanology were signals of such magnitude measured and yet nothing happened. … The volcano will probably soon be forgotten. In my memory it isn't the volcano that remains, but the neglect and oblivion in which those black people live.

The music subsides from its peak and the credits begin to roll.

Allowing for the somewhat awkward, sentimental, but honorable enough notion about poor black people, belied by the fact that we continue watching the smoking volcano for a considerable period of time, the deeper, underlying thought must be an equation of the persistence of the volcano in smoking without erupting with the persistence of the principal black man in going on living, without fear and without dying. Instead of Aguirre's naked will, there is in both cases a kind of stoic heroism in persistence and acceptance, as both the mountain and the man are what they simply are. Hence a kind of life with dignity within nature is possible, however otherwise indigent it also is, and perhaps in part because it is.

Lessons of Darkness (1992) is the second most experimental film in Herzog's career, after *Fata Morgana*. Nominally shot as a documentary about Kuwait after the first Gulf War, it in fact treats the devastated landscape mythically, that is, as a site of the unfolding of terrifying and sublime powers, largely in independence of any relation to human life, especially human social life. It is divided into thirteen sections, headed by Roman numerals, the titles of which, especially in the second half, emphasize this mythic treatment: "VI. And A Smoke Arose Like the Smoke from a Furnace. VII. A Pilgrimage. VIII. Dinosaurs on the Go. IX. Protuberances. X. The Drying Up of the Wells [*Quellen*: Sources]. XI. Life Without the Fire. XII. I am so weary of sighing; O Lord, grant that the night cometh [the title of the Bach Easter cantata '*Ich bin so müde vom Seufzen; Herr laß es Abend warden*' that plays throughout this section]". Its epigraph, attributed to Pascal but in fact written by Herzog, reads "The collapse of the stellar universe will occur, like creation, in grandiose splendor." This epigraph is shown, along with the credits, over the opening of Wagner's *Das Rheingold*: 128 measures of a arpeggiated E-flat chord, in a low register, that function as an entry into Wagner's own mythic world of the Norse-Germanic gods. The opening shot shows six gigantic concrete towers, like enormous inverted martini glasses, without evident purpose, against a dramatic orange sunset, and without any human beings in view, as Herzog intones, "a planet in our solar system ... [cutting to a mist-covered mountain range] white mountain ranges, clouds, a land shrouded in mist." Then, against a fiery background, we see two human figures—firefighters shrouded in asbestos suits—silhouetted by background smoke and flames, in the frame of what will turn out to be a heat protection shield—as Herzog tells us, "the first creature we encountered tried to communicate something to us."

Everything is presented as primeval, with no reference to the specific political history of Kuwait. Much of the action of large construction machines (the dinosaurs of part VIII) digging fire trenches and firefighters spraying streams of water onto blazing infernos seems to be presented slightly slowed down, as if to emphasize its ritual character. When there is human action, it is presented largely in long shots and in snippets without beginnings-middles-and-ends. Interspersed with the snippets of human action are scenes of lakes of oil bubbling from heat (the protuberances of part X), raging oil fires, and despoiled

Figure 5 *"The first figure we encountered tried to communicate something to us," from* Lessons of Darkness *(1992).*

landscapes. Section IV, "Finds from Torture Chambers," consists of close-up pans of instruments of torture laid out on tables, followed by a mostly close-up interview with an Arab woman who had "lost her speech but ... still tried to tell us what happened," in halting gestures interspersed with a few words, as she had watched her two grown sons being tortured to death.

In part VI, "Childhood," a mother holding her young son explains that "he hasn't spoken a word since" having his head crushed by the boot of a soldier. "Then they shot my husband." Once only after the torture and murder, the child said "Mama, I don't ever want to learn how to talk," as though language and civilization as such were not worth the price paid for them in violence and death. Part VII, "And a Smoke Arose Like the Smoke from a Furnace," consists entirely of helicopter long-shot images of smoke and fire (a cherry-picker truck briefly moves through the mid-ground of one of these), sometimes including landscapes and oil lakes, sometimes not, all set to the Funeral March from Wagner's *Götterdämmerung*. The section opens with Herzog reading from Revelations 9:1–2 and 9:6:

And the fifth angel sounded, and I saw a star fall from heaven onto the earth. And to him was given the key of the bottomless pit, and he opened the bottomless pit, and there arose a smoke out of the pit as the smoke of a great furnace, and the sun and the air were darkened by reason of the smoke. And in those days shall men seek death and shall not find it, and shall desire to die, and death shall flee from them.

The soundtrack throughout consists of sacred music or music otherwise concerned with death: not only Bach and Wagner, but also Edvard Grieg's "Death of Aase," Arvo Pärt's *Stabat Mater*, and Giuseppe Verdi's *Requieum Mass*, along with somber pieces by Mahler, Prokofiev, and Schubert. As in *Fata Morgana*, the point of view, mise-en-scène, and soundtrack suggest a post-human world or a world in which the human is only a temporary and largely unhappy, violent blip in the development of the earth. And yet, insofar as the images *are* to move us (along with the stories of the tortured) to see what we have done (and to resonate to the insight of the images themselves), the picture is perhaps not completely bleak and apocalyptic. "*Herr laß es Abend werden* [Lord, let the evening come]" at least points toward the possibility of a more religious attitude toward life, perhaps as in the dignified acceptance of death of the principal figure of *La Soufrière*.

One of Herzog's most successful but less well-known films, the documentary *The White Diamond* (2004), does a great deal to fill in what worthwhile human action might look like,[40] even while accepting the transitoriness of human life in nature. In developing this picture, Herzog achieves some of the most astonishing images of nature of his entire career. About two-thirds of the way into the

---

[40]Exactly how it does this will be treated at greater length in Chapter 3.

film, after mid-range aerial shots of the Guyanan jungle, taken from a small, two-person airship in which he has been flying as a cameraman passenger, Herzog cuts to successive extreme close-ups of a tree frog crawling across leaves, a caterpillar covered with small, oddly tree-like white branches moving on a leaf, a tree snake perhaps about to strike, a second tree frog backing down a branch and then inside its bark, a large lizard—at one point its back alone fills the entire frame—and an insect peering at the camera frontally, all set to dissonant, non-melodic music for solo cello, as though the sounds were from a prehuman, primeval epoch of the earth. Taken together, these images suggest a nature that proliferates unusual forms of life without either regard or any privilege for the human. Contrasted with these images of nature's indifferent self-development are vignettes of human beings indulging in various kinds of interesting eccentricities: building an airship to explore the jungle canopy for medicinal plants, raising chickens, break dancing above a waterfall to recorded Zimbabwean music, sending glasses of champagne tethered to balloons over a waterfall in order to test the air currents, among other things.

At the very end of the film, as two of the principal characters, lying at the edge of a cliff above the spectacular Kaieteur Falls, are talking about the swifts that live in caves behind the falls, Herzog cuts to a crowd of hundreds of swifts in flight, filling the screen as they circle around one another in the empty sky ("like there's a music controlling them")—a shot he holds for some forty-eight seconds. He shows the protagonists talking briefly, returns to the swifts against the sky for thirty-five seconds as the protagonists continue talking about them. As the camera lingers on the swifts and the protagonists continue talking, a contemporary Kyrie, composed for the Senegalese singer Mola Sylla, chorus, and cello by the cellist Ernst Reisjeger, swells up and continues throughout the ensuing shots. Herzog then cuts to the top of the falls themselves. The camera pans slowly down with the descending torrent for twenty-seven seconds, with some swifts passing in a blur in front of the falls, stopping at the spot where the falls reach the river below. The swifts against the sky reappear for eighteen seconds. Then there is a cut to what turn out to be the moss-covered cliffs above the waterfall, as the camera pans from the cliff back to the waterfall, bringing it into view from the side as the swifts circle in front of it. As the shot of the swifts circling the falls is held for thirty seconds, one has the sense of curiously mirroring natural processes, the swifts in their continuing, persistent circling answering to the water's continuing downward fall in mutual suspension. This sense is reinforced by a shot of the same scene, now held from above for sixty-two seconds. The stream of water flowing over the rock edge is visible in the upper right corner of the frame, the torrent with mists fills the frame's center, and the swifts continue to circle the torrent.

Finally, there is a cut to a roughly thirteen-second-long shot of mountains blanketed by a sea of mist, glowingly lit from above by an invisible sun behind the camera, as if to take departure from everything we have just seen. The screen fades to black, and we read brief accounts

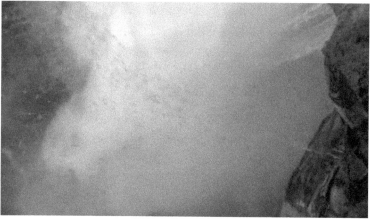

Figure 6 *The swifts circling Kaieteur Falls, from* The White Diamond *(2004).*

of what the two protagonists we have just seen are doing now, as the music fades, leaving only the sounds of the flying swifts. The words, "May the Secret Kingdom of the swifts be around till the end of time, as the lyrics to this song suggest," appear on screen. A joyous "Swift Song" for two female voices and chorus begins, and the credits roll.

It is one of the most astonishingly evocative sequences in the history of filmmaking. Visually and acoustically, the swifts in their flying and the water in its falling are equated with the oddly compulsive doings of human beings, the only difference being the addition of reflective intelligence and language on the part of the human beings. Or are these additions, given the all but obsessive eccentricities of what these figures have been doing, rather than just another aspect of nature's development that will, in time, pass the human by? There is no better filmic acknowledgment of fundamental, mysterious conditions of human life in time than this.

Grizzly Man (2005) is merciless in exposing Timothy Treadwell's naïveté about nature in general and grizzly bears in particular. Contrary to Treadwell's projections onto the bears of possibilities of reciprocity and even intimacy with him, to Herzog, again, the bears' "blank stare speaks only of a half-bored interest in food." And yet he finds a kind of meaning in Treadwell's life in virtue of his achievement as a filmmaker and his encounter with primordial nature outside the bounds of more settled life. He includes Treadwell's self-filmed proclamation that the bears saved him from alcoholism and gave him a life. "I will die for these animals. I will die for these animals. I will die for these animals. Thank you so much for letting me do this. Thank you so much for these animals, for giving me a life. I had no life. Now I have a life."

Herzog concludes the film by commenting as the voice-over narrator, over a shot taken by Treadwell of three bears running playfully and powerfully along the sandy shore of a lake:

Treadwell is gone. The argument how wrong or how right he was [about whether he was protecting the bears or whether he was, instead, mad, about whether it was right to expose his girlfriend to them, about the nature of nature as such, and about where life might be found in it] disappears into a distance, into a fog. What remains is his footage. And while we watch the animals in their joys of being, in their grace and ferociousness, a thought becomes more and more clear. That it is not so much a look at wild nature as it is an insight into ourselves, our nature. [Cut to Treadwell, accompanied by foxes, walking away from camera.] And that for me, beyond his mission, gives meaning to his life and to his death.

In this passage of narration, the "it" in the penultimate sentence is curiously referentially opaque. Is Herzog referring to Treadwell's footage? To our watching of it? To the bears themselves? To a thought becoming clear?—Somehow, arguably, all of these, as bears plus (contextualized and edited) footage plus viewing prompt thoughts about human life in nature as such.

Herzog then cuts to a close-up of the bush pilot Willy Fulton, who had ferried Treadwell into and out of Katmai National Park on the Alaska Peninsula, singing along to Don Edwards performing "Coyotes," with the plane's motion shown from left to right in the frame, by implication away from Treadwell's camp and back toward civilized life. "Now the longhorns are gone, and the drovers are gone. The Commanches are gone, and the outlaws are gone. Geronimo's gone, and Sam Bass is gone. And the lion is gone. And the red wolf is gone. And [Fulton adds] Treadwell is gone." There is a final cut to Treadwell, filmed from behind, walking away from us along a running stream, accompanied calmly by two large grizzlies just behind him. The visual effect is the thought that a life of significance has somehow been lived in and in relation to nature, whatever nature's cruelties are and whatever Treadwell's demons, inconsiderateness, and madness were. He is not a hero to be emulated, but his life has nonetheless somehow been intensely lived.

Encounters at the End of the World (2007) refers in its title to the various people Herzog has met during his filming at the NSF-run McMurdo Station Research Center in Antarctica. But Herzog also exploits the natural ambiguity of "end" to refer to a temporal as well as a geographic terminus. He picks up again the idea from *Fata Morgana* (1971), *Lessons of Darkness* (1992), and *The Wild Blue Yonder* (2005), subtitled "Requiem for a Dying Planet," of the earth as seen after the passing of the human, as if by extraterrestrial aliens. As he puts it in his narration, voiced over shots of abandoned machinery and deserted buildings (as in *Fata Morgana* and *Lessons of Darkness*):

> For this [—massive ash volcanic eruptions that alter courses of biological and cultural evolution—] and many other reasons, our presence on this planet does not seem to be sustainable. Our technical civilization makes us particularly vulnerable. There is talk all over the scientific community about climate change. Many of them agree the end of human life on this earth is assured. Human life is part of an endless chain of catastrophes, the demise of the dinosaurs being just one of these events. We seem to be next. And when we are gone, what will happen thousands of years from now in the future? Will there be alien archaeologists from another planet trying to find out what we were doing at the South Pole?

Later on Herzog shows research scientists watching the 1954 science fiction film *Them!* on television, which film he then freely re-edits out of sequence to show first a radio and television broadcaster announcing martial law, followed by the film's opening announcement of the generation of giant ants as a result of atomic bomb testing, followed by an expert entomologist commenting on what is happening, who ends with a citation from Revelations 17:8.

> Stay in your homes. I repeat, stay in your homes. Your personal safety, the safety of the entire city, depends on your full cooperation with the military authorities. ... Yes, cities, nations, even civilization itself, threatened with annihilation, because in one moment of history-making violence, nature—mad, rampant—wrought its most awesome creation. For born in that swirling inferno of radioactive dust were things so horrible, so terrifying, so hideous, there is no word to describe them! ... We may be witnesses to a biblical prophecy come true. "And there shall be destruction and darkness come upon creation, and the beast shall reign over the earth."

Alongside this apocalyptic perspective, however, *Encounters* also includes strikingly beautiful images of vast ice fields, smoking volcanos, magma lakes, and natural ice caves. The very idea for shooting in Antarctica came from Herzog's having seen underwater footage, shot by Henry Kaiser and used in *The Wild Blue Yonder* (2005), from beneath the Ross Ice Shelf (Cronin, 381). The film ends with a 1:20 sequence of underwater images—ice caves, ice chimneys, trapped air bubbles, and brilliantly colored jellyfish in close-ups—an image that will recur in *Bad Lieutenant: Port of Call New Orleans* (2009)—set to the basso profondo Russian Orthodox hymn "*Il est digne en verité*" (Verily, He Is Worthy). As Reinhold Steingröver aptly observes, this sequence "evoke[s] nature's return to its primal state after the demise of the civilized world. ... This is not an alternative environment for humans after they have destroyed their planet, but nature's return to itself"[41]—as though it were actively hymning itself, in ways that

---

[41]Steingröver, "Encountering Werner Herzog at the End of the World," pp. 466–88, at p. 482.

include but also transcend human life. This sequence is introduced by the Bulgarian "philosopher, forklift driver" Stefan Pashov, who tells us that the American Buddhist philosopher Alan Watts "used to say that through our eyes the universe is perceiving itself, and through our ears the universe is listening to its cosmic harmonies, and we are the witnesses through which the universe becomes conscious of its glory, of its magnificence."

Stanley Cavell describes "the material basis of the media of movies"—or at least photographically produced movies as opposed to cartoons or CGI—as "a succession of automatic world projections,"[42] the world itself captured on film. As Cavell argues, for a photographically produced film, as for a still photograph and unlike a painting, it always makes sense to ask "what was left outside the frame?": "the camera … crops a portion from an indefinitely

Figure 7 *An underwater ice cavern, from* Encounters at the End of the World *(2007).*

---

[42]Stanley Cavell, *The World Viewed*, Enlarged Edition (Cambridge, MA: Harvard University Press, 1979), p. 72.

Figure 8 *The philosopher-forklift driver Stefan Pashov: "we are the witnesses through which the universe becomes conscious of its glory, its magnificence," from* Encounters at the End of the World *(2007).*

larger field"[43] of the actually existent. This makes photographic film in general what Cavell calls "a moving image of skepticism"[44]—the world presented as unfolding itself for my viewing alone, without any possibility of either my intervention in it or my responsibility for it.

To the extent that a given film supports my conviction in this unfolding of the world—a slack, clichéd, or incoherent film will fail to do this—the world itself presents itself to me as meaningful (through, of course, the way in which the director of the film captures this unfolding photographically).[45] When this happens, then, as André Bazin (a crucial source for Cavell) argues, the world is presented to me "in all its virginal purity to my attention and consequently to

---

[43]Ibid., p. 24.

[44]Ibid., p. 188.

[45]For a fuller account of Cavell on the ontology of film and the distinct artistic possibilities it enables, see Richard Eldridge, "How Movies Think: Cavell on Film as a Medium of Art," *Estetika: The Central European Journal of Aesthetics* LI/VII, 1 (2014), pp. 3–20.

my love,"[46] as a place that is good enough to live in, unfolding itself meaningfully on its own, apart from my temporary place in it.[47] This is also what Herbert Marcuse calls the affirmative dimension of art, where, in and through the very estrangement from ordinary experience the artwork offers, through its succumbing to "the tyranny of form," wherein "no line, no sound could be replaced," it "reveals the essence of reality in its appearance."[48]

Herzog's major unfoldings of the natural world captured photographically—the images constructed through aiming the camera, stylized through editing, and supported by narration and score—often situated summarily at the ends of his films, and further supported by their contextual, narrative-resolving functions, are as coherent and compelling as any sequences of film images ever produced. They enable us to bear obscure perceptual witness to the fact that cathartic, resolutive meaning is at least intermittently available within life in nature, however brutal and terrible its ways also are. Through that witness, embodied in moving images and offered to us in the experience of them, we can acknowledge that temporarily circumscribed, mysterious life in nature is possible for us, however much nature's indifferent self-development also transcends both us and any discursive understanding.

---

[46]André Bazin, "The Ontology of the Photographic Image" (1945), in *What Is Cinema?* Vol. I, trans. Hugh Gray (Berkeley, CA: University of California Press, 1967), pp. 9–16, at p. 15.
[47]The idea that art in general does this (along with natural beauty) is the sense of Kant's famous claim in *The Critique of the Power of Judgment* that art engenders in suitably attentive audiences "the harmonious free play of the cognitive faculties" or an absorbed lingering in meaning felt and perceived in the presentation, apart from any particular cognitive-subsumptive judgment.
[48]Herbert Marcuse, *The Aesthetic Dimension*, trans. and revised Herbert Marcuse and Erica Sherover (Boston, MA: Beacon Press, 1978), pp. 8, 42.

3

Selfhood

Send out all your dogs and one might return with prey. … Develop your own voice. Day one is the point of no return.
—WERNER HERZOG (CRONIN, BACK DUST JACKET)

Self is one member of a tangled family of concepts, along with *substance, subject*, and *person*, that are used to describe human beings or aspects of the lives of all or most human beings. As will become clear, it is more apt to talk of *selfhood* as a status or role that most human beings acquire or fulfill to some extent rather than as an entity somehow lodged "inside" the biological human being. But in order to make this clear, it is important first to mark out the applications of the other members of this complicated family.

Substance is the most general term. It refers to more or less well-bounded, temporally continuing, space-occupying things.[1] (Is fog a substance, or is a shower of rain? Perhaps not, but a single raindrop among the many that compose a rain shower is.) Perhaps among substances some of them exist eternally and are the very stuff of the physical world—quarks, gluons, neutrinos, or some other things

---

[1] Here I follow P. M. S. Hacker, *Human Nature: The Categorial Framework* (Oxford: Blackwell, 2007), pp. 29–30. Hacker is explicating and refining the largely Aristotelian conceptual scheme that is manifested in all our thinking and uses of language.

as may be. But eternal existence is not part of the very concept of substance, and in all likelihood elementary particles pass into and out of existence individually as they transmute into each other, throw off photons, and so on under the influence of forces. Temporally and spatially bounded ordinary lumps of iron or gold, planets, acorns and tomatoes, goldfish and dogs, and ping pong balls and chairs count as *substances* in any reasonable sense of the term. Among substances, along with cats, dogs, dolphins, mosquitos, and other members of biological species, are human beings, "animate spatio-temporal continuant[s] of a certain kind,"[2] as P. M. S. Hacker puts it. In particular, like cats but unlike lumps of iron, they are living bodies that grow and develop according to biological processes.

The term *subject* has a variety of uses, so that the concept *subject* has a variety of application conditions. Most generally, it applies to anything that responds to external influences or is an object of attention or discussion. We can and do talk, for example, of being *subject* to gravitational attraction or to government authority, or of being the subject of a discussion, an essay, or an experiment. Human beings are subjects in each of these senses, in that they respond to external forces (natural, such as gravity, and juridical, such as authority) and can be objects of attention and discussion. In addition, like other higher mammals, they have spatiotemporal points of view on the world, so that they are the subjects as bearers of states of consciousness, insofar as they register the world through sensory awareness.

In addition to being both substances (bounded spatiotemporal continuants) and subjects (to influences, of attention, of consciousness), most human beings, perhaps all, are *persons*. Like *goalkeeper, second violinist,* or *professor, person* is a role, norm, or status concept.[3] It does not

---

[2]Ibid., p. 265.
[3]See ibid., p. 293.

refer to any entity separate from an individual biological human being (as substance and subject). Instead, it refers to individual biological human beings insofar as they have acquired and exercise certain responsibilities and effective powers as occupants of roles under instituted norms. For *professor*, for example, this is obvious: professors are authorized to, are expected to, and normally do construct syllabi, conduct lectures, assign and grade essays, sit on departmental committees, and so forth. Historically, the concept of a *person* developed out of the Greek concept *persona* or mask worn on stage by an actor who took on an assigned role. In the Roman world, it was used to pick out those human beings, whether citizens of the empire or foreigners, who (unlike slaves) could engage in contracts and were subject to the code of civil law.[4] From this usage, under the influence of the Christian conception of the equal dignity and worth of all human beings, its application broadened to include all normal human beings beyond a certain age, namely those who have the abilities to assess their conduct and to guide it according to norms. As Hacker puts it, *persons* are those who are "answerable for [their] deeds."[5] They are the living biologically human individuals who are aware of what they do and are able and normally apt to modify their conduct in light of expectations and norms, including familial, social, cognitive, political, or moral ones as may be. In Hacker's apt summary, "the concept of a person qualifies a substance concept of an animal of such-and-such a kind, earmarking the individual of the relevant kind as possessing (or as being of such a nature as normally possessing) a distinctive range of powers, a personality, and the status of a moral being."[6] It is perhaps an open question whether certain higher mammals such as chimpanzees or dolphins possess such powers, so that they should be counted as persons, or whether

---

[4]See ibid., pp. 286–7.
[5]Ibid., p. 312.
[6]Ibid., p. 313.

there could someday be artificial persons in the form of machines thus answerable for their deeds on the basis of awareness. But human beings beyond very early childhood remain the central and paradigm cases of beings (substances and subjects) who are persons. The concept *person* is also extended to include infants, who in the course of normal subsequent development will become explicitly able to answer for their deeds, and to human beings with radical defects from which, it can be hoped (as it always can be), they might yet recover. Finally, there are the artificial *persons* of the law: corporations, townships, civic associations, and the like, who are able through their designated representatives to enter into contracts, are subject to civil and criminal laws, and who are in general answerable for what they do.

In contrast with each of these concepts—*substance, subject,* and *person*—the concepts of *self* and *selfhood* are more tangled and confused. Historically, the word *selfa* appears in Old English as a term of emphasis, used not to refer to any entity, but instead to stress that some entity otherwise already identified is the very subject at issue, as in "Thys is the thing selfe that is in debate" (Sir Thomas More 1532), where "thing selfe" means "the very thing."[7] Once, however, with the rise of modern physical science nature was disenchanted, so that it came to be seen typically as nothing but collocations of material atoms, then the term migrated to begin to refer, mysteriously and confusedly, to some "inner" and yet nonphysical entity that is the subject or bearer of consciousness, volition, and other psychological processes and states. After all, if nature or the world of existing things is nothing but disenchanted, physical atoms, and yet there are such things as consciousness, volition, hope, despair, pain, and joy, then these phenomena must have some bearer other than the

---

[7]Ibid., 261–2.

"mere" physical body as mechanism. This is the source of Descartes's account of the mind as a non-physical something that is the bearer of processes of thought, consciousness, and will. Looking within, Descartes argues, we can discover the existence of "what we are" as an inner thing that thinks, in complete independence of physical-material states and processes.

> Examining *what we are*, while supposing, as we now do, that there is nothing really existing apart from our thought, we clearly perceive that neither extension, nor figure, nor local motion nor anything similar that can be attributed to body, pertains to our nature, and nothing save thought alone. ... By the word thought, I understand all that which so *takes place in us* that we of ourselves are immediately conscious of it; and, accordingly, not only to understand (INTELLIGERE, ENTENDRE), to will (VELLE), to imagine (IMAGINARI), but even to perceive (SENTIRE, SENTIR), are here the same as to think (COGITARE, PENSER).[8]

On the face of it, this account makes little sense. How can there be a non-material, non-space-occupying bearer of any properties, psychological or otherwise? What are the criteria of identity for such things, and how are they to be counted, if they take up no space? How could such things interact causally with physical things? Under the pressures, however, of the physicalist-materialist picture of nature, of the more or less self-evident fact that we do think and feel things, do deliberate and choose, and of the sense of inwardness

---

[8]René Descartes, "The Principles of Philosophy," in *Discourse on Method, Meditations, and Principles*, trans. John Veitch (London: J. M. Dent, 1994), Part I, Principles VIII–IX, p. 153; emphases added. Descartes argues for the claim that the mind and the body are distinct substances (in virtue of having distinct primary or defining attributes that are fully conceivable apart from each other) in *Meditations* VI and *Principles* LXIII.

and detachment from the course of the world that comes from having to engage in long periods of education and training, involving distantiated reflection and inhibition, before one becomes fluent within the frameworks of modern scientific and technical practices, the picture of "outer" material world and "inner" non-material something persisted. There is a complicated range of asymmetries between the conditions, frequently subject to dispassionate, isolated observation and measurement, for attributing material qualities (mass, charge, velocity, etc.) to physical bodies and the conditions for attributing psychological, volitional, characterological, affective, perceptual, and cognitive features to human beings.[9] If these features are real, then they must have a bearer, and if that bearer cannot be the merely mechanical human physical body, then, so it seems, it must be an inner, nonphysical mind or self or something. Locke regards the biological human individual as the spatiotemporal substance that is somehow the indirect bearer of these features. But he also posits a direct bearer—a mental entity or extra "being" somehow "within" the biological human animal—that he calls the *person* or *self*.

> We must consider what *person* stands for;—which, I think is a thinking intelligent being, that has reason and reflection and can consider itself as itself, the same thinking thing, in different times and places. … When we see, hear, smell, taste, feel, meditate, or will anything, we know that we do so. Thus it is always as to our present sensations and perceptions: and by this everyone is to himself that which he calls *self*.[10]

---

[9]See Hacker, *Human Nature*, pp. 272–6 for a survey of these asymmetries.

[10]John Locke, *An Essay Concerning Human Understanding* (New York: Dover, 1959), Vol. I, Book II, Ch. xxvii, Section 11, pp. 448–9.

Again, the postulation of an "inner," "nonspatial" entity makes little sense. No further bearer of thoughts, feelings, attitudes, emotions, sensations, and processes of reasoning and choice is either necessary or apt over and above the living human animal. But as an *experience* a sense of being present to oneself, with one's mental life somehow private to oneself and hidden from others, is very common. We can keep our thoughts and feelings to ourselves for the most part, at least beyond early childhood. (Lying and dissembling are learned arts, but they are normally learned.) Especially in modern technological cultures with their long periods of schooling, wherein one is forced to inhibit one's natural responses and to monitor and correct one's performances over an extended period of time, it is easy to feel that one *has* one's mental life, in the form of a set of shifting thoughts, feelings, attitudes, and senses of possibility and power, somehow housed within and problematically awaiting this expression. Adolescence with its natural awkwardnesses heightens this feeling.

Thus even if there is no bearer of a distinctly self-conscious and conceptually structured mental life over and above the human animal, there remains a sense of this life as being somehow inside, both as an object of present experience and reflection and as somehow awaiting expression. Uniquely, human beings have richly contentful, structured attitudes toward who they are. As Hacker usefully summarizes the self-conscious, reflective, and anxiety-ridden character of human life, in contrast with the lives of other animals:

> Human beings have, and can know, a history. ... They can dwell lovingly, proudly or guiltily upon their lives. ... Only human beings can dwell on, and in, the future and the possibilities it holds. Animal life is full of fear; human life is also full of hope. Only human beings are aware of their mortality, can be occupied or preoccupied with their death and the dead. We are unique

among animals in being able to strive to understand our lives and the place of death in life.[11]

Or, as Heidegger famously put it, human being is the kind of being for whom "its very Being ... is an issue for it."[12]

What is the source of this distinctive form of life, with its powers of reflection, senses of possibility and power, and openness to anxiety? Surely the biological evolution of complex human brains able to store and process enormous amounts of information is a necessary condition for having the relevant mental life that includes consciousness, self-consciousness, reflection, and deliberation. It is less clear that that evolution is by itself sufficient. We lack a full story that explains how mental states, processes, and powers are nothing but physical processes, and insofar as the attribution conditions for mental states, in being holistic and subject to constraints of reasonableness, are different from the measurement-based attribution conditions for physical states, there is some reason to think that no such story will be forthcoming.[13]

Aristotle filled this explanatory gap speculatively by arguing that human beings are rational animals: bits of living substance that are specifically formed or organized so as to have rational powers of intellect and deliberation. These rational powers exist first in human beings as capacities or potentials (*dynamis*). They then become explicit abilities or actualities (*energeia*) as a result of appropriate socialization and training. For example, I am born *capable* of speaking Urdu—I have the potential or implicit capacity (*dynamis*) to do this, insofar as

[11]Hacker, *Human Nature*, pp. 237–8.

[12]Martin Heidegger, *Being and Time* [1927], trans. John Macquarrie and Edward Robinson (Oxford: Basil Blackwell, 1962), p. 32.

[13]See Donald Davidson, "Mental Events," in *Essays on Action and Events*, ed. Davidson (Oxford: Oxford University Press, 1980), pp. 207–24.

I am a member of the species of language-mongering animals—but I am not *able* to speak it. I have not been trained or socialized in Urdu, and I don't know a word of it. Hence I lack the actuality (*energeia*) of Urdu speaking.[14]

To this descriptively plausible picture, Aristotle then adds the descriptive-normative thought that it is the purpose (*telos*) or completion (*entelechia*) of any living body that its distinctive powers be actualized. An acorn does not flourish or become what an acorn should be unless and until it successfully actualizes its distinctive powers of growth (with the help of normal conditions) and grows into an oak tree. Likewise, according to Aristotle, a human being does not flourish unless and until it successfully actualizes its distinctive rational powers appropriately. A human life without actualized rational powers is a wasted, tragic, unfortunate, or otherwise non-flourishing one. There are many forms of practice within which rational powers can be actualized: Aristotle lists friendship, art, music, politics, science, and philosophy as among the most important ones. We would surely extend this list further to include democratic citizenship, participation in family life, meaningful work, and sports, among many other things.

Whatever its descriptive accuracy and charms, however, Aristotle's account is speculative and ungrounded in modern physical science, which eschews talk of powers. More important, however, human life, and especially modern human life in societies with highly differentiated forms of labor, is more complex and contested than Aristotle took Greek male aristocratic life to be. It is difficult for many to see how to enter into and to sustain a meaningful life when

---

[14]Aristotle distinguishes *dynamis* and *energeia* in Aristotle, *Physics*, trans. R. P. Hardie and R. K. Gaye, in *The Basic Works of Aristotle*, ed. Richard McKeon (New York: Random House, 1941), Book VII, Ch. 4, p. 365.

there are both significant material scarcities and complex, contested forms of specialized labor and social reproduction. As a result, all but continuously during adolescence, wherein one prepares for entry into adult life under conditions of uncertainty, and at some moments during later life, more or less everyone lives with a sense of inner powers and potentials as not fully actualized and expressed and of the significance of one's life as not fully recognized. We think of our *selfhood* as the combination of our distinctive inner personality and powers, as what is somehow most essential to us, and as somehow private or sealed within us. Wordsworth memorably expresses this sense of inner powers unactualized and of having a life that is somehow stunted and unsatisfying as he describes himself as "Baffled and plagued by a mind that every hour/Turns recreant to her task; takes heart again,/Then feels immediately some hollow thought/ Hang like an interdict upon her hopes."[15] Stanley Cavell finds this sense of selfhood unactualized—collapsed, as it were, into an inner subjectivity—to be generally shared in modern life. "We wish," as he puts it:

> For the power to reach this world, having tried for so long, at last hopelessly, to manifest fidelity to another. ... At some point the unhinging of our consciousness from the world interposed our subjectivity between us and our presentness to the world. Then our subjectivity became what is present to us, individuality became isolation. ... Apart from the wish for selfhood (hence the always simultaneous granting of otherness), I do not understand the value of art.[16]

---

[15]William Wordsworth, *The Prelude* [1850], in *Selected Poems and Prefaces*, ed. Jack Stillinger (1965), Book I, ll. 257–60, p. 198.

[16]Stanley Cavell, *The World Viewed*, Enlarged Edition (Cambridge, MA: Harvard University Press, 1979), pp. 21–2.

In having this unsatisfied wish for selfhood, we worry "that we are not free, not whole, and not new, and we know this and are on a downward path of despair because of it," with the result that we then hope "we might despair of despair itself, rather than of life, and cast *that* off, and begin, and so reverse our direction."[17] Selfhood is experienced as a status to be achieved, through actualization of personal-impersonal hidden powers. Failing in that achievement, it can seem as if one haunts the world, with one's bodily motions as nothing but mysterious reflexes of physical-social processes, or one can try to take revenge on the world through narcissistic violence.

While these are arguably extreme reactions to a sense of failure to sustain the expression of rational powers within one's course of life, they are nonetheless possibilities that continuously surround the lives of human subjects as such and that may come into play to various degrees at any moment. In his Anthropology and Phenomenology, the first two subsections of his theory of subjective spirit or individual mind, Hegel provides a compelling developmental ethology for human beings as animals with rational powers, according to which these possibilities remain continuously in play.[18] According to Hegel, there is such a thing as "the self-possessed and healthy subject" who "has an active and present consciousness of the ordered whole of his individual world, into the system of which he subsumes each special content of sensation, idea, desire, inclination, etc., as it arises, so as to insert them in their proper place."[19] Such subjects, one might

---

[17]Cavell, *The Senses of Walden: An Expanded Edition* (San Francisco, CA: North Point Press, 1981), pp. 60, 71.

[18]For a fuller sketch and assessment of Hegel's developmental ethology, see Richard Eldridge, "Hegel's Account of the Unconscious and Why It Matters," *The Review of Metaphysics*, LXVII, 3 (March 2014), pp. 491–516.

[19]Hegel, *Philosophy of Mind*, Part Three of the *Encyclopedia of Philosophical Sciences*, trans. William Wallace and A. V. Miller (Oxford: Clarendon Press, 1971), §408, p. 73.

say, know what they are doing and feeling, and why, as active, self-conscious agents within an ordered world, able to distinguish what is trivial and incidental from what is really important. Nonetheless, Hegel is clear that the process of becoming such a healthy subject is an unfinished one that admits of lapses, as rawer bodily and psychic phenomena assert themselves in one's life against the grain of healthy normalization.

> In consequence of the element of corporeality which is still undetached from the mental life, and as [self-]feeling too is itself particular and bound up with a special corporeal form, it follows that although the subject has been brought to acquire intelligent consciousness, it is still susceptible of [psychic] disease, so far as to remain fast in a special phase of its self–feeling, unable to refine it to "ideality" and get the better of it. ... When the influence of self-possession and of general principles, moral and theoretical, is relaxed, and ceases to keep the natural temper under lock and key, the earthly elements are set free – that evil which is always latent in the heart, because the heart as immediate is natural and selfish. It is the evil genius of man which gains the upper hand in insanity, but in distinction from and contrast to the better and more intelligent part, which is there also. Hence this state is mental derangement and distress. The right psychical treatment therefore keeps in view the truth that insanity is not an abstract loss of reason (neither in the point of intelligence nor of will and its responsibility), but only derangement, only a contradiction in a still subsisting reason.[20]

Even healthy psychic and practical life is surrounded by fantasy and at least tendencies to both vengeful narcissism and despair, as one

---

[20]Ibid., §408, p. 73.

lives, especially in a less than fully well-ordered public social world, with a sense of selfhood unexpressed and of social normalization as victimization.

Since the process of developing integrated, expressed selfhood housed within a coherent, meaningful social role takes place, insofar as it is possible, not only in the life of a corporeal subject, but also in interaction with other such subjects—Hegel emphasizes the role of the mother—who also seek selfhood's expression, the result is a process that inherently involves contestation and struggle. "In that other as ego I behold ... an immediately existing object, another ego absolutely independent of me and opposed to me. ... This contradiction gives either self-consciousness the impulse to show itself as a free self, and to exist as such for the other: – the process of recognition. The process is a battle."[21] For beings such as we are—embodied subjects who seek the expression of selfhood within worldly practice fraught with conflict—innocence and freedom from reflection are not finally possible.

In both his documentaries and his fiction films, Herzog continuously investigates a range of cases involving both the achievement and the defeat of the expression of selfhood in forms of worldly practice. These forms include not only madness and withdrawal, but also experiences of striking self-presence in bodily activity. Typically, what attracts Herzog's interest is *not* the ordinary stuff of family life or commercial life, but instead either efforts to break through to new forms of bodily self-presence, against the normalizing demands of social life, or, more broadly, lives that are somehow cast out of ordinary circuits of shared activity. As Dana Benelli aptly remarks, "he accords transcendent value to

---

[21]Ibid., §§430–1, p. 78.

lives lived in keeping with alternative (that is, non-traditional or 'uncivilized') forms of consciousness, regardless of the literal outcome of those lives."[22] More specifically, his protagonists, in S. S. Prawer's formulation, are "outsiders in a society where they can never feel at home, and which in the end destroys them; and rebels who try, by violent means, to realise what their lives refuse them but also ultimately fail."[23] Or as Paul Cronin puts it, "we are repeatedly confronted with dispossessed outcasts and eccentrics, estranged loners, struggling overreachers and underdogs who live *in extremis*, at the limits of experience, isolated and fraught with problems of communication and assimilation, railing against sometimes stifling social conventions, often foolhardy and spirited enough to embark on undertakings they know are futile."[24] Herzog himself describes his protagonists in similar terms.

I have always felt that my characters all belong to the same family, whether they be fictional or non-fictional. They have no shadows, they are without pasts, they all emerge from the darkness. I have always thought of my films as really being one big work that I have been concentrating on for forty years. The characters in this huge story are all desperate and solitary rebels with no language with which to communicate. Inevitably they suffer because of this. They know their rebellion is doomed to failure but they continue without respite, wounded, struggling on their own without assistance.[25]

---

[22]Dana Benelli, "The Cosmos and Its Discontents," in *The Films of Werner Herzog*, ed. Corrigan (London:Routledge, 1986), pp. 89–103, at p. 91.

[23]S. S. Prawer, cited in Paul Cronin, "Visionary Vehemence: Ten Thoughts about Werner Herzog," in Cronin, pp. xi–xli, at p. xxiv.

[24]Ibid., p. xxiv.

[25]Herzog, *Herzog on Herzog*, ed. Paul Cronin (New York: Faber and Faber, 2002), p. 68; compare Cronin, p. 79.

Herzog equates communication with convention, bureaucracy, routine, and administered order, against which he poses subjectivity as a locus of unexpressed powers, owing to handicap, victimization, madness, or narcissism. Thomas Elsaesser observes that "communication in his films is impersonal: more like lifting luggage onto a train than exchanging information. [In contrast], subjectivity is nothing other than the effect of a resistance to signification, and especially to language as transparency."[26] Whatever this resistant subjectivity is, however, it is for Herzog largely a subject of interest and admiration rather than diagnosis and explanation. The films work at

> blocking … any easy interpretation of [their principal figures] as sociological case studies, [at enacting] a refusal to have the handicapped, the blind or the sick become subsumed under the discourses of institutionalized medicine, charitable religion or the welfare worker, before they have a chance to appear first and foremost as human beings. Instrumentalized politics is rejected by Herzog in the name of human dignity.[27]

Rejecting diagnosis and explanation, Herzog instead pays close attention to what his outsider figures actively *do* in detail. They have either chosen or been forced into efforts to make meaning and express their powers of selfhood in the face of a hostile administered social world. Thinking especially of the documentaries—of the mute figures of *Land of Silence and Darkness* (1971), *Ballad of the Little Soldier* (1984), and *Lessons of Darkness* (1992), of the inspired preaching of Huie Rogers and Gene Scott, and of the competitive auctioneers in *How Much Wood Would a Woodchuck Chuck* (1977), William Van

---

[26]Thomas Elsaesser, "An Anthropologist's Eye: *Where the Green Ants Dream*," in *The Films of Werner Herzog*, ed. Corrigan (London: Routledge, 1986), p. 144.
[27]Ibid., p. 150.

Wert usefully divides the forms of resistance to administration on the parts of their protagonists into silence, dialect, and babble, arguing that "Herzog is searching, almost in the manner of a folklorist, for the last poetry possible, and for a language, or a refusal of language, that merges with music."[28] To this taxonomy of resistance, we can add the maniacal projects of Aguirre and Fitzcarraldo, the heroic recoveries from catastrophes of Dieter Dengler and Juliane Koepcke, and the physical achievements in extreme situations of Walter Steiner and Reinhold Messner.

These various figures function, for Herzog and for viewers, as foci of identification and vehicles for exploration of the expression of powers of human selfhood in a world that is otherwise mad or empty of sense. Herzog makes this point at length in one of his most important summary statements about his work.

There is nothing eccentric about my films; it's everything else that's eccentric. I never felt that Kaspar Hauser, for example, was an outsider. He might have been continually forced to the sidelines, he might have stood apart from everyone, but he's at the true heart of things. Everyone around him, with their deformed souls, transformed into domesticated pigs and members of bourgeois society, they are the bizarre ones. Aguirre, Fini Straubinger and Stroszek all fit into this pattern. So do Walter Steiner, Hias in *Heart of Glass*, Woyzeck, Fitzcarraldo, the Aborigines of *Where the Green Ants Dream* and the desert people of *Fata Morgana*. Look at Reinhold Messner, Jean-Bédel Bokassa, Nosferatu, and even Kinski himself, or Vladimir Kokol, the young deaf and blind man in *Land of Silence and Darkness* who connects with the world only

---

[28]William Van Wert, "Last Words: Observations on a New Language," in *The Films of Werner Herzog*, ed. Corrigan (London: Routledge, 1986), pp. 51–71, at p. 55.

by bouncing a ball off his head and clutching a radio to his chest, much like Kaspar, who plays with his wooden horse. None of these people are pathologically mad. It's the society they find themselves in that's demented. Whether dwarfs, hallucinating soldiers or indigenous peoples, these individuals are not freaks.

… I have a great deal of sympathy for these people, to the point where Jörg Schmidt-Reitwein joked that I should play everyone in my films myself. I function pretty well as an actor and in several of my films could have played the leading character if necessary. I could never make a film—fiction or non-fiction— about someone for whom I have no empathy, who fails to arouse some level of appreciation and curiosity. In fact, when it comes to Fini Straubinger in *Land of Silence and Darkness*, Bruno S. in *The Enigma of Kaspar Hauser* or Dieter Dengler, these people are points of reference not just for my work, but also my life. I learnt so much from my time with them. The radical dignity they radiate is clearly visible in the films. There is something of what constitutes them inside me. (Cronin, 78–80)

As with all major art, we—human beings in general—and the expression of our powers of selfhood are what are centrally under investigation, for Herzog and for the viewers. What is sought is disclosure of what our defining human powers are and how they might be more effectively exercised (both within the action of a film and in the making of the film itself) than they mostly are. In taking up the human subjects of his films, Herzog argues, in a 1979 conversation with Roger Ebert, that:

It's exactly the same that is done in chemistry when you have a particular substance that is unknown to you. When this happens, you must put this substance under extreme conditions—like extreme heat, extreme pressure, extreme radiation—and it is only *then* that you will be able to find out the essential structure of this substance which you are trying to explain and to discover and to describe.

RE: That, in a sense, is what happened in *Aguirre, the Wrath of God.*

WH: In almost *all* of the films.[29]

In the documentaries directly concerned with religion—*God's Angry Man* (1980), *Huie's Sermon* (1980), *Bells from the Deep* (1993), *The Lord and the Laden* (1999), *Pilgrimage* (2001), *Wheel of Time* (2003), and *Happy People* (2010)—Herzog considers human beings as they respond to the specific pressures and possibilities of religious ritual and entry into a fuller, more meaningful human life. Religion for Herzog is not centrally a matter of doctrine or belief in propositions. Instead it takes the form of what Pierre Hadot calls spiritual exercises, involving

> a concrete attitude and determinate life-style, which engages the whole of existence. [A spiritual exercise] is not situated merely on the cognitive level, but on that of the self and of being. It is a progress which causes us to *be* more fully, and makes us better. It is a conversion which turns our entire life upside down, changing the life of the person who goes through it. It raises the individual from an inauthentic condition of life, darkened by unconsciousness and harassed by worry, to an authentic state of life, in which he attains

---

[29]Herzog, *Herzog by Ebert*, p. 9. See also p. 124: "I am curious about our human condition. As you would understand the very nature of physical natter by putting it under extreme temperature, pressure, or radiation, similarly human beings would reveal their nature under extreme conditions. The Greeks have a proverbial saying I always liked: 'A captain only shows during a storm.' Ordinary lives are the ones we lead, but they are not really a fertile soil for movies." Compare Cronin, p. 25.

self-consciousness, an exact vision of the world, inner peace, and freedom.[30]

The contours, promise, attractiveness, and possibility of such a conversion of a way of life from within a way of life are what Herzog is centrally concerned to investigate.

Such possibilities of conversion present themselves in two interrelated forms: a performer's wholehearted immersion in a leading role, involving mastery of repeated verbal motifs and their cadences in order to hold the attentions of an audience, and an audience responding to presentations of the sacred. The first form is most prominent in Herzog's two 1980 films about preachers: *God's Angry Man* [in German: *Glaube und Währung—Dr. Gene Scott, Fernsehprediger; Faith and Currency—Dr. Gene Scott, Television Preacher*] and *Huie's Sermon*. Gene Scott is a Southern California televangelist who spends thirty hours each week doing live television to solicit donations. "God's honor is at stake every night. This is not a show. It's a feast—the Feast of the Fading Experience." The film consists of shots of Scott on set, with the television cameras visible, haranguing his audience to donate more money, more often, intercut with shots of his Christian studio band, close-up interviews with Scott in his limousine and office, and with his parents. There is no voice-over, and there is no intervention from Herzog except in the form of brief, off camera questions that he puts to Scott. We see Scott stalking about the set and fuming in silence in between his outbursts. We learn that in addition to his television show he is also responsible for two churches, a mausoleum, a travel agency, and a real estate firm. Yet Scott owns nothing personally, he tells us, except a small black

---

[30]Pierre Hadot, *Philosophy as a Way of Life: Spiritual Exercises from Socrates to Foucault*, trans. Michael Chase (Malden, MA: Wiley-Blackwell, 1995), p. 83. Compare the discussion of Hadot on spiritual exercises in Chapter 1 above.

briefcase with straps that he carries about with him at all times, whose contents he will not reveal. "My simple dignity of privacy is restricted to that bag." He is unable to have children, having been rendered sterile by mumps as a child. Herzog tells us that the film stemmed from the fact that:

> whenever I was in America I would always switch on his programmes, and quickly became addicted. As wild as he might have been as a public figure, there was something heartbreaking about him that moved me. He could never have been a friend of mine, but I still somehow liked him. He was basically a one-man show, on screen for up to eight hours every day. (Cronin, 181)

The film ends with a shot of Scott's FCC Monkey Band—a set of some twelve or so windup toy monkeys playing cymbals and drums and swinging on a trapeze bar, shown in relative close-ups, both as a set and individually, in a way that emphasizes their strangeness and Scott's mania in using them. (Scott had been feuding with the FCC about whether his show counted as a tax-exempt religious enterprise.) This is followed by a close-up of a male singer, and then a cut to the opening of Scott's television show: the title *Festival of Faith* in large letters, set against the Los Angeles skyline, backed by a female Gospel singer, singing "Maybe you haven't heard about it, but there's a stranger in our town. Oh yes there's a stranger in our town, " followed by an announcer intoning "Dr. Gene Scott presents the *Festival of Faith*. Not a lot of Hoopee; just straight talk. Now, here's your host" as the screen then fades to black.

Throughout the presentation of Scott is generally neutral— midrange on set shots and close-up interview shots, in which Scott talks freely. Yet the interjections of the parents—his mother describes him sneaking chocolate frosting as a two-year-old, for which she slaps his hand, inducing a tantrum, and then dunks him under a cold faucet—of the unusual, often off-key Christian music, and especially of the FCC Monkey Band suggest an ironic distance. Herzog is here evidently finding something attractively individual in Scott's obsessions and also something oddly off about him, thus leaving open the question about how distinctively individual personality and shared rational powers might be best or better exercised.

Huie's Sermon (1980) is even more direct in its presentation than *God's Angry Man*. It opens with a shot of the front of The Greater Bible Way Temple, a Black Apostolic Church in Crown Heights, Brooklyn. We see parishioners entering for a worship service, followed by a cut to a shot of a Bible illustration of Jacob's dream of a ladder to heaven, as if to raise the question what sort of ascent within or from ordinary life might be possible. We then see the interior of the church from the rear, as the choir moves into place as they "step to Jesus." The remainder of the movie focuses continuously on Pastor Huie Rogers, as he delivers his sermon on the text of Colossians I:15–16, 18. Colossians I:16 reads "For by Him were all things created, that are in heaven, and that are in earth, visible and invisible, whether they be thrones, or dominions, or principalities, or powers: all things were created by Him, and for Him" (KJV).

Pastor Rogers opens with "there's a lot wrong with the world. There's a lot wrong with society. There's a lot wrong with the neighborhood. There's a lot wrong with the community. Jesus is all right." He then proceeds to catalogue the world's ills, including homosexuality, sperm banks, eugenics, and surrogate pregnancies. "Man has become so presumptuous that he feels that he himself has become a god. Everything that man made has perished. Everything that man puts his hand to is corruptible." He promises elevation—being raised up into heaven bodily—through trust in Jesus. "You will be raised up. In the air. Present in the resurrection." The sermon is unscripted. Pastor Roberts moves freely across the front of the church. Call and response occur frequently. "Tell somebody Jesus is all right. Yeah. ... Can you say amen?" The tempo increases steadily, with occasional brief pauses for Huie to gather energy. (Compare James Brown, who developed his style from the Black Apostolic Church, and compare the tempo of the auctioneers in *How Much Wood Would a Woodchuck Chuck?* [1976]). Clapping, chanting, rim shots, and then percussion riffs and organ join in. Elders lay hands on members of the congregation as Huie preaches.

There are two brief cuts away from the service, each about one minute long, about half way through (21:03) and just over three quarters of the way through (33:51). Both are traveling shots taken from a car moving through the streets of Crown Heights, showing abandoned lots, derelict boarded-up buildings, parked cars, and sidewalks with grass growing though them. At 38:00, there is a minute-long shot from the interior front of the church, as we see baptisms taking place in a large pool high up on its interior rear wall. At 39:08, there is a mid-range shot of Pastor Roberts, now in a regular suit rather than his pastor's robes. With bustling noises in the background, he blinks several times and nods slightly, while looking straight at the camera in silence.

As he does so, the text, taken from *Huie's Sermon*, but translated into German, appears in large yellow letters in the foreground: "*Wenn der Mensch etwas mit der Sonne zu schaffen hätte, wäre sie heute nicht aufgegangen*" ("If man had anything to do with the sun, it wouldn't be rising every morning, nah".) The text disappears, and the shot is held for another fifteen seconds. Then there is a cut to black and the credits begin.

What have we witnessed? There are evidently experiences of rapture and transport out of the ordinary, both for Huie and for his flock. The sermon and the congregation's response to it are presented straight, without irony. At the same time, the interjected traveling

Figure 9 *Huie Rogers gazes into the camera, from* Huie's Sermon *(1981).*

shots seem to suggest either that poverty and dereliction cause this form of religious practice or that this practice cannot be trusted if it fails to address these conditions. Yet it does not quite say either of these things, and the issues of whether this practice can be trusted, by whom, for what reasons, and in what circumstances remains open. Where is Jacob's ladder? Herzog reports having had an intense religious experience himself at the age of fourteen.

> There was a dramatic condensation of everything in my life at the time and a need to connect to something sublime, but my interest in religion dissipated and dwindled away fairly quickly … though to this day there is something of a religious echo in my work. [But] the scientific basis of reality will always be more important. … The facts are facts. (Cronin, 3)

Once again, Herzog is interested in what one might call the grammar of elevation into meaningfulness, as it becomes available, whether trustworthily or not, to various people in various circumstances. Taken together, his various investigations of religion reveal the force and multiple shapes of the desire for elevation as it presents itself in the lives of many—a desire the force of which Herzog seems to feel even while being uncertain which, if any, of its shapes to trust.

This is equally true of the religious documentaries that concern participant response somewhat more than the practices of leading performers (the boundaries are not everywhere clear). Herzog typically focuses on audience experiences of a sacred object or setting as itself a kind of intense bodily performance. As Eric Ames aptly observes about *Bells from the Deep* (1993), but in a remark that applies equally well to *Pilgrimage* (2001) and *Wheel of Time* (2003), "Herzog foregrounds the sensuous relationship between the physical body of the believer and the venerated image. Spirituality is exteriorized, made sensuous and tangible, through the believer's interaction with the unseen image. It is this relationship that constitutes the actual subject of the film."[31]

God and the Burdened, also known as *Christ and Demons in New Spain* (1999) was commissioned as part of the BBC series *2000 Years of Christianity*. Herzog chooses as his subject the radically syncretic devotional and ritual practices of Guatemalan native Indians. The film opens and closes with an Easter procession in Antigua, Guatemala, featuring swinging censers, purple satin robes, a statue of Jesus on the cross being carried through the streets, and later on further processors in black robes and in white robes with large pointed white hoods. In between we see men at

---

[31]Eric Ames, *Ferocious Reality*, p. 94.

work carrying heavy loads of wooden poles and boards, laden baskets, and large bales of cloth on their backs. We visit the Church of San Simon/Maximon—a saint figure represented as a chain-smoking Spanish ranchero who is the patron saint of drinking, cigar smoking, and male sexuality—in the highlands village of San Andrese Sepa. In the village we see men, women, and children smoking enormous cigars and women practicing cleansing rituals that involve spitting water on one another and slapping each other with water-drenched foliage. Some larger historical context is provided by shots of Codices housed in Paris and Florence that recount in both images and text the brutal conquest of Mexico by Cortes. Toward the end, a preacher describes "the profound anxiety of the human being who feels abandoned, helpless, and despondent" as it is symbolized by Jesus on the cross. The film ends with the narrator telling us that there is "a visual way of conveying a message," adding "at this moment, quite without words, we will receive a message" as we see shots of a painted wooden statue of the crucified Jesus, stigmata and blood fully in view, being carried into the church on a bier and then adjusted into the proper position by elders, all set to Orlando di Lasso's 1580 *Missa pro defunctis.* Throughout, the emphasis is on the odd, syncretic things that these people are intensely doing, in response to "the collapse of their world" through conquest and massacre that has left them "disturbed individuals to this day." Issues about propositional belief or theological doctrine are not raised, other than to ask, "What are they doing? Who is their Jesus?" Here, too, as in both *God's Angry Man* and *Huie's Sermon*, Herzog is evidently attracted to what these people do (especially to their intense involvements in "a visual way of conveying a message") yet also apart from them.

Bells from the Deep: Faith and Superstition in Russia (1993) offers the widest range of religious phenomena in the documentaries. It opens with a famous and famously staged shot—Herzog hired drunks in order to film the scene and told them what to do—of three men crawling across the ice of the frozen Lake Svetloyar listening for the bells of the lost sunken city of Kitzeh in central Russia. Following this opening, we meet a Mongolian Tuva throat singer shown in close-up against an ice-floe saturated flowing river. We come across an isolated ramshackle wooden village, where the camera moves inside to show a shaman chanting, praying, and preparing tea for a cleansing ceremony. Vissarion—Jesus the Redeemer returned to earth—preaches and baptizes believers. Alan Chumack, Faith Healer, transmits cosmic positive energy to charge water and ointments with ions. Yuri Tarassov, Sorcerer and Exorcist, carries out exorcisms. The elderly bellringer, Yuri Yurevitch Yurief, orphaned as a child, tells the story of his past and performs on the bells, pulling and stepping on strings. The second half of the film concentrates on people and stories having to do with Lake Svetloyar: a man and a woman who crawl about the lake individually, prostrating and crossing themselves, and kissing the ground, a man who immerses his head in the lake; stories about a vision of a cathedral, spirits, bells, and a choir at the lake, about an attacking pig, and about a sacred stump that can heal the sick. Toward the end, Vissarion the Redeemer preaches, and a basso profundo begins to sing on the soundtrack. As the basso continues, there is a cut to a sequence of medium long shots, lasting 1:43, of ordinary people skating and fishing on the lake. Two skaters with their hands behind their backs move in tandem away from the camera. A single skater zooms into and out of the frame from right to left, then from left to right. These last shots have the feel, again, of a kind of interested but generally neutral leave-taking: we have seen the sorts of things religious people in Russia do. As Eric Ames notes, throughout

> Herzog foregrounds the embodied aspect of religious devotion as displayed by other people. The camera in *Bells from the Deep* tends to single out individual bodies, faces, and gestures, while the editing and the music suggest connections among the different images that appear on-screen. We see churchgoers crossing themselves; worshipers drinking consecrated water and venerating relics; pilgrims crawling on their hands and knees; "the Redeemer" touching the disfigured hands of a follower; a group of middle-aged women sobbing, some of them screaming, as an exorcist goes about his work on stage.[32]

Wonder and interest, though not endorsement, predominate over explanation. As Herzog himself puts it in commenting on his use of the camera in *Wodaabe, Herdsmen of the Sun* (1989), in a remark that applies equally to all his religious documentaries.

> I purposefully pull away from anything that could be considered anthropological. In the opening scene of the film the tribesmen are rolling their eyeballs, extolling the whiteness of their teeth, making these ecstatic faces, and on the soundtrack over these images you hear Gounod's "Ave Maria", a recording made in 1901 and sung by the last castrato of the Vatican. ... Using the aria means that the film is not a "documentary" about a specific African tribe, rather a story about beauty and desire. (Cronin, 214)

Just so for the use of the basso profundo and Russian Orthodox hymns in *Bells from the Deep*. In general, "what matters," as Ames puts it, "is

---

[32]Eric Ames, *Ferocious Reality: Documentary According to Werner Herzog* (Minneapolis, MN: University of Minnesota Press, 2012), p. 92.

the patterned repetition of ritualistic acts. Showing these patterns and thus exploiting the film medium's own basis in repetition becomes a strategy for making visible what Diana Taylor has described in another context as 'performance's capacity to reforge belief through reiterated behaviors.'"[33]

Pilgrimage (2001) is an eighteen-minute film that alternates between shots of pilgrims near the tomb of Saint Sergei in Zagorsk, Russia (taken from *Bells of the Deep*) and pilgrims to the Basilica of Guadalupe in Mexico City. It presents close-ups, sometimes extreme ones that show rapt unfocused gazes of the faithful crossing themselves, walking on their knees toward shrines, and kissing statues. There are occasional interjections of shots of the rocky edge of Christmas Island in the Indian Ocean filling the foreground, with waves crashing against it behind, as if to suggest eternal repetition. The film has no text or voice-over narration. The sound track consists entirely of a liturgical-sounding score by the contemporary British composer John Tavener, with repeated, drawn-out, quickly modulating, *Sprechstimme*-like intoning of Mahámátra (Sanskrit: Great Mother) and Theotokos (Greek: Mother of God) set in front of slowly modulating minimalist chords.

Wheel of Time (2003) follows the painstaking construction of two sand mandalas, one of them as part of the twelve-day Kalachakra initiation in Bodh Gaya, a ceremony through which 500,000 meditators attempt to purify themselves of greed, hatred, ignorance, and envy. Some of the faithful undertake 100,000 prostrations each in front of the tree where the Buddha was enlightened. Others touch

---

[33]Ibid., pp. 92–3, citing Diana Taylor, "Remapping Genre through Performance: From 'American' to 'Hemispheric' Studies," *Publications of the Modern Language Association* 122, 5 (2007), pp. 1416–30, p. 1418.

and rub their backs against a column believed to have healing powers. One monk has traveled 3,000 miles to Bodh Gaya, taking three and a half years, prostrating himself at each step. Close-ups of the faithful meditating, praying, prostrating themselves, cooking, and jostling for consecrated barley dumplings are prominent. Thousands of pilgrims undertake an arduous three-day, fifty-two-kilometer high-altitude purification trek, including prostration points, around the base of the sacred Kailash mountain, the seat of Lord Shiva. The film ends with a shot of one monk, sunk in prayer, amid 400,000 now empty pillows of the faithful in Bodh Gaya, followed by fifty seconds of shots, presented in silence, of Lake Rakshastal shimmering in front of Mount Kailash, then of the mountain itself, as if the camera were taking summary leave of the human, leaving behind only the larger nature that surrounds temporary human life.

In all the documentaries concerned directly with religion, the focus is on repeated bodily religious doings, often in extreme form. Herzog's attitude is consistently that of engaged, yet evaluatively neutral wonder at the fact that people do these things, as they lead their lives out of neither instinct nor the conventions of modern life, but instead out of passionate commitment sustained in and through repetition. The epigraph to *Pilgrimage* (2001), ascribed plausibly to the fifteenth-century German mystic Thomas à Kempis, but in fact written by Herzog (Cronin, 347), reads "it is only the pilgrims who in the travails of their earthly voyage do not lose their way, whether our planet be frozen or scorched: they are guided by the same prayers, and suffering, and fervor, and woe." Evidently, for Herzog, one must, in order to achieve selfhood and a sense of meaning more fully, be underway passionately, as if on a quest for the sacred. Drift, stale convention, and anomie are the enemies of the achievement of human selfhood; passionate bodily engagement in repetition is its necessary condition of possibility.

Herzog's major fiction films typically focus on a single protagonist who is radically ill-suited to the prevailing conditions of social life. It is hard to imagine Herzog making a romantic comedy that concludes in a happy marriage, the traditional figure of successful integration into the social world. This focus on maladjustment is equally true of Herzog's less compelling fictions: *Fitzcarraldo* (1982), *Cobra Verde* (1987), *Invincible* (2001), *The Wild Blue Yonder* (2005), *Rescue Dawn* (2006), *Bad Lieutenant: Port of Call—New Orleans* (2009), *My Son, My Son, What Have Ye Done* (2009), *Queen of the Desert* (2015), and *Salt and Fire* (2016). The difference from the more compelling fictions is that in the minor cases the maladjustment is either less clearly motivated, less sympathetic, less consistently expressed and explored than in the major successes, or some combination of these. For example, Fitzcarraldo's obsession with opera is simply posited as a discrete fact about him, unconnected with his conditions of life as an Irish would-be entrepreneur living in a small city in the Amazon basin. Other than from Kinski's rapt expressions, we can't tell why or, more importantly, how he cares about opera. Terence McDonagh in *Bad Lieutenant* suffers from a bad back that leads to addiction to Vicodin and cocaine and thence to disaster, but we see little texture or struggle to his descent. Nicole Kidman, an otherwise fine actress, is ill-suited to play Gertrude Bell in *Queen of the Desert*: her quick, urbane emotional and social intelligence undermines the plausibility of the character's entrancement with desert life. The ecologist Dr. Laura Sommerfield in *Salt and Fire* is kidnapped and then stranded together with two blind children on barren, rock strewn salt flats, by a mad CEO whose motivations are unclear. (Does he want a false report of the ecological disaster his consortium has caused or a true one? Apparently a true one, it turns out, but then why the coercive kidnapping?) Once there, she does little but suffer and survive. The aliens in *The Wild Blue Yonder* and the voice of God (with his face later present on a Puritan Oats container) during a Peruvian kayak trip in *My Son, My Son, What Have Ye Done?* are both portentous but failed devices for reaching after a significance that the narrative and the images fail to bear.

With the major, compelling successes, things are quite otherwise. Even when the cases are as extreme as Aguirre's crazed will or the minor, chaotic riotings of the dwarfs in *Even Dwarfs Started Small* (1970), the treatment and expression are consistent, and there is something in the obsessions of the central figures with which one can identify. Paul Cronin suggests that Herzog's principal characters (fictional and nonfictional) can be divided into those who "brazen[ly] seek overwhelming challenges" and "victims … who have burdens thrust upon them."[34] Brad Prager divides them similarly into grand-scale madmen (Aguirre, Fitzcarraldo, Timothy Treadwell) or those who deliberately set themselves against the ordinary and minor-scale madmen (Stroszek, Kaspar Hauser, Woyzeck) or those who more passively find themselves caught in impossible circumstances.[35] These divisions are apt enough, but they are all but true by definition—some are more active; some are more passive—and they do not yet capture the specific textures within which these figures coherently live out their estrangements from ordinary social life.

Commenting on Herzog's first major feature film, *Signs of Life* (1968), Brigitte Peucker provides a useful general characterization of the terms of Herzog's theme of opposition between the individual and the social.

---

[34]Cronin, "Visionary Vehemence," p. xxiv.

[35]Brad Prager, *The Cinema of Werner Herzog: Aesthetic Ecstasy and Truth* (London: Wallflower Press, 2007), Chapter 1 is entitled "Madness on a Grand Scale"; Chapter 2 is "Madness on a Minor Scale."

When ... Stroszek [in *Signs of Life*] is confronted with 10,000 turning windmills whose movement resembles that of the minnows he has watched swimming in circles, he feels as though the landscape were mocking him and he responds by going mad. He challenges the sun with fireworks, believing that "one can only counteract light with light", as long as it is dark, Stroszek's fireworks, his signs of life and of rebellion, seem to have conquered. But then the dawn outshines his fire. As futile as it is titanic, Stroszek's challenge is an attempt to meet nature upon its own terms, to "speak the language of nature," to come to terms with it by means of immediate, natural signs rather than the arbitrary signs of writing, like those of Becker's tablets.[36]

That is, for Stroszek, as, it will turn out, for Herzog's other major figures, convention and social authority, thought of as coercive and represented by language, are set in opposition to nature and internal powers of self-making, represented by ecstatic visuality that calls forth internal powers. (It is no accident that so many of Herzog's principal figures, especially the more active ones, fictional and nonfictional,— Aguirre, Fitzcarraldo, Graham Dorrington, Reinhold Messner, Fitzcarraldo, and Timothy Treadwell—seem to be director surrogates in responding to landscapes and the power of visual experience of them.)

Without this consistent general thematic structure—convention, social authority, and language versus nature, internal power, and visuality—the events of some of the films would otherwise feel unconnected. Like his companion soldiers Meinhard and Becker uselessly guarding an abandoned fortress on the Greek island of

---

[36]Brigitte Peucker, "Literature and Writing in the Films of Werner Herzog," in *The Films of Werner Herzog*, ed. Corrigan (London: Routledge, 1986), pp. 105–17, at p. 108.

Cos during the Second World War, and like his wife, Nora, Stroszek in *Signs of Life* (1968) is bored. But why does he rather than these others go mad? The immediate cause of his madness is the sight while he is out on patrol with Meinhard of 10,000 windmills rotating beautifully, perhaps manically, in an arid valley. This suddenly provokes him to begin firing his rifle in the air repeatedly and pointlessly. Soon thereafter he collapses into paranoia—the military authorities are thinking of sending him away—chases off his companions with his rifle, barricades himself in the fortress, and begins setting off the fireworks they have previously made for their amusement out of old munitions. Why does he do this? Some viewers have found this madness unmotivated. But it is crucial that just before the scene with the windmills we have seen Stroszek successively (1) captivated by a pianist whom he has stumbled across playing Chopin in the town—a composer whom the pianist calls malicious [*bösartig*] and unpredictable [*unberechenbar*]— (2) asking his commandant in town for something more to do because he feels "closed in somehow [*eingeengt*]" by the walls of the fortress, (3) walking on patrol with Meinhard, (4) encountering a poor farmer and his young daughter, who "can almost not speak," but who, awkwardly twisting her dress while seated, haltingly sings a song about mountain lambs grazing in loneliness. Successively, these experiences seem to intimate to him that there is no place in the world for him and his powers. He cannot express himself through music (a signature emblem of human animation for Herzog), he is closed off from expressive interactions with others, and the young girl in her awkwardness seems to show the difficulties and pains of coming to even partial expressiveness. What is left for him turns out to be nothing but aimless setting off of fireworks. Yet these amount to achievements of visuality on which the camera lovingly dwells in its penultimate 1:32 sequence, backed by a lyrical cello-guitar duo, and to something in which, Stroszek, we are told, had "found his true calling" so that "no one could touch him [*keiner könne ihm etwas anhaben*]." "At ten he was already catching trout with his bare hands, while other boys were still wetting their pants"—an image of superior intimacy with nature in the exercise of human powers. Finally, he is captured and carted off, presumably to an institution. A dream or fantasy of fullness in the expression of human powers against the grain of a stultifying ordinary has been defeated. As Dana Benelli comments about the progress of the film as a whole, comparing it with *Aguirre*:

> Both *Signs of Life* and *Aguirre* literally begin in voids—one with an image of an expanse of rather nondescript terrain, the other with clouds. Then the camera responds to a movement in the environment, a 'sign of life' generated by the presence of people in the framed space. In a sense, this is a moment of 'birth' for the character whose experience the viewer will watch and follow to a concluding situation in which that individual's fate is undeniably materialized, recognized and ordained.[37]

As we see dust rising from a dirt road, shot from the rear interior of the truck in which Stroszek is being taken away, we are told that "in his rebellion he had undertaken something titanic, for the enemy was far superior. Thus he had failed as miserably as all others of his kind." Caught up as we have been in the camera's responsiveness to landscape and to the fireworks, at this point we may feel that we, too, are all of his kind, at least insofar as we likewise undertake or wish to express our natural human powers of selfhood more fully than the norm but mostly fail in doing so.

---

[37]Benelli, "The Cosmos and Its Discontents," p. 92.

Even Dwarfs Started Small (1970) is on the face of it a film about a minor rebellion that escalates into minor chaos, taking place in some sort of training institution for dwarfs on the Canary Islands (though all speak German). It seems to explore the occasions, varieties, attractivenesses, and costs of rebellion in general allegorically, but it offers no external references to decode the allegory. It opens with a mid-range, objectifying shot of Hombre, the smallest of the male dwarfs, sitting in a high chair, between two windows set in a white wall, aimlessly turning a metallic stencil of what must be an inmate's identification number. After a 360-degree pan across a landscape including stucco-ed, institutional buildings with very small windows, we see first a chicken pecking and eating the corpse of a second chicken, and then further Antonioni-like shots of landscapes and blowing trees, before the camera settles on a long-shot aerial view of the institution, with labels for the functions of its various buildings. (If one wishes to search for influences, one can find traces of both Antonioni's cinematography and Tod Browning's [*Freaks*, 1932] uses of dwarfs, as well as a plot that somewhat resembles William Golding's 1954 novel *Lord of the Flies* [film version 1963].) The camera returns to Hombre, who is being told how to sit for a police photograph. He turns his head to look out the window, and the camera follows and shares his gaze. Hombre is told to confess, and at this point the entire rebellion unfolds in flashback, apparently through Hombre's memory, or Hombre's memory objectified in the camera, as he is interrogated, prefaced by his "No, I won't tell you."

What ensues are a variety of hijinks involving sexuality, violence, and in general the unleashing of libidinal energies. Hombre and the smallest female dwarf are forced by the others to "marry," but Hombre proves unable to climb into the bed to which they have been sent. All enjoy the pinup photos that have been left by one of the absent authorities. Reacting against the instructor—another dwarf who has barricaded himself indoors against the rebellion, together with a dwarf prisoner—who announces that "Cleanliness and Order is our Motto," the dwarfs break windows, smash dishes, engage in a food fight, kill a nursing sow, and arrange a chicken fight. Intermittently throughout we see pecking chickens, two blind-deaf dwarfs (or perhaps children) wearing goggles, who sword-fight aimlessly with long poles and play a ball game, and a driverless car circling in a courtyard. Various dwarfs laugh excessively, sometimes without apparent cause. The film ends with a shots of a kneeling, defecating camel and then of Hombre laughing at it. Midway through the film, one of the dwarfs announces, "When we behave nobody cares. But when we are bad nobody forgets." This seems to declare the thematic point of the film as a whole. Without the ability to express libidinal energies (here as a result of institutionalization, but perhaps in general), one's life is neither one's own nor memorable. Something in the dwarfs and in us resists what presents itself as arbitrary, coercive normalization.

This thought is central to the action of *Aguirre: The Wrath of God* (1972), Herzog's masterpiece. The puzzle of the film is why we care at all about Aguirre or remain involved with him, as his relentlessly self-centered, evil will drives the entire expedition ceaselessly toward extinction. In a posthumous fragment, Nietzsche provides part of an answer: "The highest human being is to be conceived as a copy of nature: tremendous superabundance, tremendous reason in the individual, squandering itself as a whole and *indifferent* to the squandering."[38] As in Mozart's *Don Giovanni*, the continual assertion of will is more important than deference to ordinary norms of morality and decency.

---

[38] Nietzsche, *Werke: Kritische Gesamtausgabe*, eds Giorgio Colli and Mazzino Montinari, Vol. VII, Part 2, *Nachgelassene Fragmente* (Berlin: de Gruyter, 1974), Notebook 25, Fragment 140, p. 47; English translation in Adrian del Caro, *Grounding the Nietzsche Rhetoric of Earth* (Berlin: de Gruyter, 2004), p. 64.

Homer's Achilles—a central point of reference for Nietzsche in his rejection of Socratic morality and return to Homerism—is another figure of will who in his fury against Hector (a figure of civilization and settled life) inspires our awe.

> And Achilles went for him, fast, sure of his speed
> as the wild mountain hawk, the quickest thing on wings,
> launching smoothly, swooping down on a cringing dove
> and the dove flits out from under, the hawk screaming
> over the quarry, plunging over and over, his fury
> driving him down to beak and tear his kill——
> so Achilles flew at him, breakneck on in fury
> with Hector fleeing along the walls of Troy,
> as fast as his legs would go.[39]

Absent widespread, lived acceptance of either Christian metaphysics, with its morality of benevolence and charity, or something of comparable force, we are likely to resonate somewhat to the attractions of naked will and power, even while also feeling dismay and horror. Aguirre orders Perucho to rain cannon fire at nighttime on the men stranded on a raft caught in an eddy on the opposite side of the river, in order to save the trouble of either rescue or burial. Against Don Ursua, the appointed commander of the expedition, who proposes to turn back to Pizarro and civilization, Aguirre replies, "and I say, we can conquer for ourselves [*auf eigene Faust*]," as he takes over control. He orders the looting and burning of a native village and then the execution by hanging of Don Ursua. Throughout Kinski as Aguirre radiates barely suppressed intensity, fury, and energy in his contorted

---

[39]Homer, *The Iliad*, trans. Robert Fagles (London: Penguin, 1990), Book XXII, ll. 322–30, p. 550.

body, as he pursues his mad dream of pure self-founding—"I, the Wrath of God, will marry my own daughter and with her I'll found the purest dynasty the earth has ever seen"—to the very end, in the face of the answering overpowering presence of the jungle (and with the support of the air of inevitability that is contributed by the Popol Vuh score). His relentless will to self-creation is part of the very energy of the human, however else we might also wish for it to be moderated and more successfully expressed.

Kaspar Hauser and Stroszek—Cronin's "underdogs who live *in extremis*"—are the inverses of Aguirre. The social world, its conventions, and its brutalities leave them little room for the assertion of their wills, except in brief poetic moments that are free of social control. As Steingröver observes, *The Enigma of Kaspar Hauser*, in German *Jeder für sich und Gott gegen alle* [*Every Man for Himself and God against All*] (1974):

> chronicles the tale of the wild child, Kaspar, and society's failure to provide a livable environment for him. Kaspar's civilizing process occurs through language acquisition and simultaneously represents the beginning of his inevitable demise. ... By introducing the abstraction of language into the non-lingual world of Kaspar, the irreversible process of nature's alienation has begun, ending in Kaspar's death.[40]

The civilizing process begins as Kaspar, having been kept isolated in a dark cellar, is forced by a man whom he calls Father to repeat the sentence "I want to be a gallant rider like my father was before me," before the father figure carries him on his back across fields and deposits him in the town square of Nuremburg. Kaspar himself

---

[40]Reinhild Steingröver, "Encountering Werner Herzog at the End of the World," in *A Companion to Werner Herzog*, ed. Prager (Oxford: Wiley-Blackwell, 2012), p. 472.

becomes well aware that his language-learning and socialization have not been beneficent. "It seems to me that my coming into this world was a terribly hard fall," he tells Professor Daumer. He frequently uses linguistic formulations that describe things happening in or to him, passively ("*Mir kommt es vor*: it seemed to me;" "*Es hat mich geträumt, daß*: it dreamed me that") rather than verbs of first-person agency. In general, the various authorities who would socialize him—the church, the aristocracy, doctors, the police—act coercively, with no regard for the flow of Kaspar's feelings, thoughts, or interests. As he runs out of a church service, Kasper tells us that "the song of the congregation seems to me to be a disgusting appearance. And when the people stop, then the priest up front starts screaming." When in a conversation with a priest Kaspar says that the idea of divine creation ex nihilo makes no sense to him, the priest replies, "You simply must believe. Exact investigation of obscure objects of faith is wrong." Early on, when the civil authorities complain that "he's costing us a pretty penny" to house, feed, and investigate him, he is then put on public display at a fair, as one of four great riddles of the world. Kaspar is more comfortable with the young children Julius, who teaches him words, and Anna, who teaches him a nursery rhyme, than with adults. He prefers feeding small sparrows at a window to taking to the ways of the world.

On several occasions, Kaspar displays a form of natural intelligence that the public world is ill-prepared to understand or accept (as in his resistance to ex nihilo creation). He responds to the puzzle of how to distinguish a perfect truth-teller from a perfect liar not with the expected counterfactual question ("If were to ask you whether you came from the liar's village, would you say 'yes'?"—a truthteller would say "no"; a liar "yes") but instead with the brilliant, "I would ask him if he is a tree frog." Forced to declare his thoughts to a large party of aristocrats, one of whom, Count Stanhope, may adopt him, he says, "Your Grace, nothing lives in me but my life." He learns to play a Mozart waltz on the piano, awkwardly, but when forced to do so at the party, he feels unwell and withdraws to knit by himself—"an uncultivated occupation" according to Stanhope, who now rejects him.

Visually, the alternatives to coercive socialization are provided by images of a man rowing across a placid river, with blowing grasses and two women watching, that open the film and recur throughout, by an image of an undulating field of green wheat (with the epigraph printed over it, "Don't you hear that horrible screaming all around you that men ordinarily call silence?" taken from Georg Büchner's novella fragment *Lenz*), and by Kaspar's dreams (which we are shown) of the Caucasus and of a Berber caravan traveling through a desert. In all these cases, motion as a figure for more fully achieved selfhood is presented as more natural than it mostly is within codified social routines. The film as a whole raises but wisely does not answer the question to what extent socialization and naturalness might be compatible, so that one as an individual with natural personality and instincts might live decently well within a social role. As Roger Ebert aptly remarks in his 1974 review, "the last thing Herzog is interested in is 'solving' this lonely man's mystery. It is the mystery that attracts him."[41] The film ends when, after an autopsy of Kaspar, which has found a "remarkable abnormality" in his brain, "overdevelopment of the cerebellum" and "a deformity of the cerebrum," the scribe who has been taking notes on the procedure announces, as he is walking home away from the camera, "what a wonderful, what a precise report this will make! … Finally we have an explanation for this strange man;

---

[41] Ebert, "The Enigma of Kaspar Hauser," in *Herzog by Ebert*, ed. Ebert (Chicago, IL: Chicago University Press, 1979), pp. 139–42, at p. 140.

one will never be able to find a better one." The irony is unmistakable. The mysteries of the human, if they are to be captured at all, have dramatic itineraries that must be represented narratively, as in this film, not in scientific reports.

Stroszek (1977) is closely connected with *Kaspar Hauser* both in casting and thematically. Bruno Schleinstein, who had played Kaspar, now plays Bruno Stroszek, and Clemens Scheitz, who had played the scribe in Kaspar Hauser, now plays Bruno's neighbor, Mr. Scheitz. *Stroszek* was written specifically for Bruno, a Berlin street musician who had spent much of his life in orphan homes, reform schools, and prisons. In his review of the film, Vincent Canby describes Bruno as a "small, curious personality imprisoned within a large, stocky, man-sized body that seems too big for him, a vehicle that can maneuver with only the utmost effort and concentration."[42] Herzog reports that:

> *Stroszek* was built around Bruno. It reflects my knowledge of him and his environment, his emotions and feelings, and my deep affection for him. … The scenes in Berlin of him singing and playing the accordion show exactly what he would do every weekend. Bruno knew the courtyards and alleyways of the city, and some of the songs he sings in the film he wrote himself. The place where he goes immediately after leaving prison is his local beer cellar, where everyone knew him, and all the props he uses in the film—including the musical instruments—were his own. (Cronin, 155)

Thematically, as in *Kaspar Hauser*, "the community-building spirit of music," as Rembert Hüser puts it, "is thoroughly threatened by a structurally violent society."[43] (The neighbor, Mr. Scheitz, plays

---

[42]Vincent Canby, "Herzog's Pilgrims Hit the Road," *New York Times*, July 13, 1977, p. C14.
[43]Rembert Hüser, "Herzog's Chickenshit," in *A Companion to Werner Herzog*, ed. Prager, pp. 445–65, at p. 454.

Beethoven's *Moonlight Sonata,* and music seems to be the basis of the friendship between him and Bruno.)

The movie opens with Bruno being released from prison—"Because Bruno is now entering freedom [*Denn der Bruno, der geht jetzt in Freiheit*]," Bruno tells us in the third person, after blowing the odd, four-belled street bugle that has just been returned to him by the prison authorities. The issue will then be: does a commercial society that accords formal, legal freedom to its members also enable meaningful life for them, especially for such marginal figures as Bruno? The answer is not pretty. In Berlin, Bruno is bullied by pimps who resent his helping his friend, the prostitute Eva, and forced to kneel on top of his grand piano, head down, wearing largish bells on his head and rear, in order to stand as a bizarre Christmas ornament for the pimps' amusement. When Eva is beaten by the pimps, Bruno and she decide to accompany Scheitz to America, where he has a nephew in Wisconsin.

Things scarcely go better there. Bruno's mynah bird, Beo, is confiscated by customs authorities. After some encouraging sightseeing, including the Empire State Building, that shows the trio in freer motion, they make their way to Railroad Flats, Wisconsin. Bruno gets a job working as an assistant in the auto repair shop of the nephew, Clayton, and Eva works as a waitress in a truck stop restaurant. They buy a prefabricated home on credit. But there is not enough money, and things close down around Bruno and make little sense to him. He shows Eva a small sculpture of twisted metal and tells her:

> Here you see a schematic model I have made of how it looks inside Bruno. They're closing all the doors on him, and oh so politely. Now we're in America, and I thought everything would be better and we would finally reach our goal. But no. Bruno's getting pushed

aside as if he didn't exist. Now you act as if you don't even know me anymore.

Eva: Nobody kicks you anymore.

Bruno: No, not physically. Here they do it spiritually.

Bruno contrasts the harsh punishments he had received in institutions in Germany with what is happening to him now in America. "Today they do it differently. They do it like this or like this [miming beatings]. They do it ever so politely and with a smile. It's much worse. You can smell it in the air, and you can see it, too." Eva will no longer sleep with him, and she ultimately runs off with truckers whom she had been servicing in their trucks outside the truck stop restaurant. In one of the most moving, signature images, the prefabricated home is auctioned off, then towed off out of the screen from left to right, leaving only a small dog in the middle ground, another mobile home on the left, and occupying the bulk of the screen nothing but the empty prairie, with a line of trees at the horizon. The feeling of emptiness, loss, and incomprehension is overwhelming.

Left without a home and without Eva's earnings as a prostitute, Scheitz and Bruno attempt to rob a bank. When it turns out to be closed, they rob the grocery store next door, netting thirty-two dollars. Scheitz is captured by the police in the store, leaving Bruno to steal and drive off in the auto shop tow truck. He arrives at a run-down mountain resort in Cherokee, North Carolina, in misty fall weather, along with his rifle and a frozen turkey from the grocery store. In an echo of *Even Dwarfs Started Small,* Bruno sets the tow truck to run in a circle in the parking lot and carries the rifle and turkey through the tourist shop to a ski lift in the back. He figures out how to turn on the lift, and he climbs on a chair with the sign "Is this really me?" on the back.

Figure 10 *Stroszek on the chairlift: "Is this really me?" from* Stroszek *(1977).*

We see him complete a turn through the chairlift mechanism at the bottom and head up again. As the camera pans from his car up the slope, leaving him out of the frame, we hear a gunshot, presumably Bruno's suicide. We cut to a police officer in the parking lot, standing near the tow truck now in flames, who radios in "we're out here on Route 380. We've got a truck on fire, I have a man on the lift, and we are unable to find the switch to turn the lift off and can't stop the dancing chicken. If you send us an electrician, we'll be out here standing by. Over." And then, backed by Sonny Terry's harmonica version of "Old Lost John," we see perhaps the most famous image in all of Herzog's work: an extreme close-up of the dancing chicken in its coin-operated glass case in the tourist shop. Herzog holds the shot for 1:08, cuts briefly to close-ups of a drum-playing duck and a fire-engine riding rabbit, and then returns to the chicken for another twenty-three seconds, until it leaves the screen to the right and the image fades to black. The sequence suggests that we share a bizarre automatism with animal life that is both natural (the chicken dancing as a chicken on a hot or electrified surface will) and coerced (the mechanism is coin-operated). Like the chicken, Stroszek has done what it is in him to do in the natural and cultural circumstances in which he has somehow found himself. The manic celebratory harmonica suggests meaning, at least to an observer of Stroszek's life and viewer of the film, but tells us nothing about what it might be. Somehow music might inform natural and social life, but perhaps at best intermittently, without evident purpose, and under coercion, especially in a cruel commercial world.

Both *Heart of Glass* (1976) and *Nosferatu* (1979) work similar thematic terrain, but with less relentless and compelling consistency than *Aguirre, Kaspar Hauser*, or *Stroszek*. "Most of Herzog's best films do nothing less than challenge the hubris inherent in the concept of civilized life, and *Heart of Glass* is no exception,"[44] Jeremy Heilman writes. Here the hubris takes the form of an attempt to discover the lost formula for the handicraft manufacture of the ruby glass that has sustained an eighteenth-century Bavarian town but has now been lost with the death of the master glass-blower, Mühlbeck, and the burning down of the factory. The formula for the ruby glass represents an object of arcane knowledge that might enable the community to reproduce itself: "The ruby glass must save us," the factory owner desperately hopes. As Alan Singer puts it, "the inhospitality of the [ordinary] world is thus conquered in the displacement of desire to another [in the thought that something lost or hidden might save us],"[45] as though the lost formula were a

---

[44]Jeremy Heilman, "Review of *Heart of Glass*," May 2, 2002, moviemartyr.com, archived at http://www.moviemartyr.com/1976/heartofglass.htm.

[45]Alan Singer, "Comprehending Appearances: Werner Herzog's Ironic Sublime," in *The Films of Werner Herzog*, ed. Corrigan (London: Routledge, 1986), p. 193.

metaphor for the will of God or philosophico-religious ideologies in general that in fact serve only to distract their adherents from material conditions.

Yet the film does not suggest that we can or should live without desire or ideology, in clear and direct consciousness of material conditions alone. The desperate factory owner and inhabitants dig up the glass-blower's house and consult a prophet, Hias, but the formula remains undiscovered. The factory owner kills his maid in the hope that adding her blood to the silica, soda ash, and limestone might do the job. As in *Kaspar Hauser*, the idea that scientific knowledge alone might save us is subjected to criticism, as one of the suggestions that leads nowhere is that someone might read Mühlbeck's brain in order to find the formula. Hias roams the mist-covered Bavarian mountains, gazes at cows, and looks "into the distance to the end of the world," represented by bubbling pools and plunging cataracts. Notoriously, most of the cast was hypnotized for the production, and their actions throughout have the feeling of automatisms. The film ends with Hias's vision of a rocky island in the Atlantic (Skellig Rock), "on the far edge of the inhabited world." Four men set out in a small rowboat "to see if there is really an abyss" at the end of a world that they believe to be flat. Perhaps because they are moving across a calm sea as a result of their own commitments and bodily exertions, "it may have seemed like a sign of hope that the birds followed them into the vastness of the sea," an over-title informs us. Within the film, hope seems to be invested in self-induced motion across the sea and away from settled life.

Nosferatu the Vampyre (1979) treats vampirism as a release from stultifying ordinary life, but into obsession and a longing for a death that will not come. Klaus Kinski plays the vampire with consummate world-weariness and pain. Jonathan Harker, played by Bruno Ganz, is a real estate agent sent to Count Dracula in Transylvania from

Wismar, Germany, in order to negotiate the sale of a large house near Wismar. As he receives his commission from his employer, Renfield, Jonathan remarks, "it'll be good for me to get out of the city ... to get away from these canals ... that flow nowhere except always back on themselves." After being infected by the vampire, Jonathan hurries to Wismar in order to save his wife, Lucy. Upon his arrival, however, he fails to recognize her. Meanwhile, Dracula, too, arrives in Wismar, along with a shipment of his rats that bring a devastating plague. Dracula visits Lucy in her bedroom. "Stars spin and reel in confusion," she tells him. "Time passes in blindness. Rivers flow without knowing their course. Only death is queerly sure." Dracula replies that "dying is cruelty against the unsuspecting. But death is not everything. It is more cruel not to be able to die." During the next day, Dr. Van Helsing arrives to find Lucy's sister Mina dead. He tells Lucy, who rushes in:

> I don't know exactly what happened. She was already dead when I arrived. He [Jonathan] lost his sanity over it; he raved. We will study this matter systematically and scientifically, without prejudice and without superstition.
>
> Lucy: Enough with your science. I know now what I have to do.

This turns out to be offering herself to Dracula that night, knowing that "if a pure hearted woman diverts his attention from the cry of the cock, the first light of day will kill him." Dracula seems accepting, even desirous, of the death that comes to them both. Freed by a maid from a circle of crumbs of the consecrated host, arranged by Lucy, that had protected him, Jonathan, transformed into the new vampire, orders her, "bring me my horse. I have much to do. Now." We see him ride off across a desert with blowing sand, backed by the "Sanctus" from Gounod's *Solemn Mass for Saint Cecilia*. Though motivated significantly by visual and stylistic considerations—a wish to recover and modify F. W. Murnau's expressionist style in his 1922 *Nosferatu*—the argument of the film seems to be that the distinctively human, inexplicable, essentially intermingled powers of sexual desire, fantasy, and meaning-making cannot be readily housed within the routines of ordinary life, if at all. To experience them fully is to be driven out of the ordinary world, either into death with Lucy and Dracula or into a desert wasteland and an unearthly mission with Jonathan. In lacking even momentary poetic consolations, it is perhaps the bleakest of Herzog's films.

Many of Herzog's documentaries that are not directly concerned with religion focus significantly on a single isolated, fanatically committed, or eccentric protagonist, often in extreme circumstances involving substantial danger: the ski jumper Walter Steiner, the mountain climber Reinhold Messner, the plane-crash survivors Dieter Dengler and Juliane Koepcke, the airship inventor Graham Dorrington, and the grizzly man, Timothy Treadwell. This interest in single extreme cases is prefigured not only by the fiction films *Aguirre, Kaspar Hauser*, and *Stroszek*, but also by the 1971 documentary *Land of Silence and Darkness* that examines the lives of a group of deaf-blind: the children Harald and Vladimir, born deaf-blind, the uncommunicative Else Fährer, who had been warehoused in mental institutions, Heinrich Fleischmann, a deaf man who became blind at age thirty-three, after the death of his wife, and, especially, Fini Straubinger, who fell down stairs at age nine, and who then slowly became blind by age fifteen and deaf (with 5 percent hearing) by age eighteen. We meet most of the other characters as we follow Fini to congresses for the treatment of the deaf-blind, a deaf-blind zoo excursion, a visit to an arboretum, and an airplane flight. (The film is subtitled *From the Life of the Deaf-Blind Fini Straubinger.*) Herzog himself connects his interest in Fini directly with his interest in Bruno Schleinstein (*Kaspar Hauser, Stroszek*) and other figures of resistance:

Those are people in which a fire is burning that glows, and one can see this from far away. This can also be seen in Bruno, this strong light from within. In both of them [Bruno and Fini], there's this radical dignity that they radiate, and this radical quality is due to the suffering they have gone through. They give off a radiance, like one once painted saints with haloes in the late Middle Ages. That is how I see it with such people.[46]

Herzog's cinematography in shooting their faces in close-ups, as they present themselves as altogether unaware of the camera, because blind, is reminiscent of Carl Dreyer's close-ups of Renée Jeanne Falconetti in *The Passion of Joan of Arc*, as the camera seems to track emanations of resistance from within into the face.

Many images are memorable: the deaf-blind hand-spelling or touching a cactus for the first time, Harald being guided into a swimming pool, and Vladimir hitting himself with a ball, then throwing and retrieving it, as he moves about and purses his lips to make a buzzing noise. As Randall Halle remarks about Vladimir, "the fact that Vladimir is oblivious to us allows us to peer at him without entrapment, but it also leads us to feel shut out from his interior life. He appears engaged with a world to which we have no access. We can peer at his face and his actions all we want, but there is no point of translatability."[47] That is, Vladimir and the deaf-blind in general seem here to sustain themselves within circuits of activity, thought,

---

[46]Herzog, Gregor, Hohlweg, and Jansen, eds, *Herzog/Kluge/Straub* (Munich: Carl Hanser, 1990), p. 127; cited in English in Gertrude Koch, "Blindness as Insight: *Land of Silence and Darkness*," in *The Films of Werner Herzog*, ed. Corrigan, pp. 73–86, at p. 76. Compare Cronin, pp. 79–80.

[47]Randall Halle, "Perceiving the Other in *Land of Silence and Darkness*," in *A Companion to Werner Herzog*, ed. Prager, pp. 487–509, at pp. 507–8.

and feeling to which we have no access, and the film seems to regard this as a kind of heroism. As Halle puts it, "Herzog's films operate according to a motto, it is not the person that is bizarre but rather the society in which he or she lives that makes them so."[48] "If a worldwide war were to break out now, I wouldn't even notice it," Fini tells us.

The film ends with an astonishing 4:08 sequence that begins with Heinrich sitting on a bench, outside the home for the elderly where he lives, between Fini and his aged mother who are talking. Heinrich rises, Fini shakes his hand, and he begins to wander about the courtyard, with his back to the camera, as the controlled, intense third movement Largo of the Vivaldi Cello Concerto in E-minor comes up on the soundtrack. Heinrich encounters a tree, and he painstakingly feels its branches, as he explores his world tactilely. He drifts away from the tree and picks up a few leaves, as the Vivaldi soundtrack continues to increase steadily in volume. His mother retrieves him and takes him by the hand into the entrance of the home. The camera pans up to the spire on the top of the building, then down to a medium shot of Fini—the conscience and center of consciousness of the film—standing under a tree, framed by foliage, as the Largo reaches its final cadence. Fini's remark about not noticing a world war appears in white letters on a blue-black background. Herzog focuses on this sequence in particular, one that he simply captured with "no preconceived structure," in his comments on the film that describe it as "some of the best work I've ever done" (Cronin, 85).

> The shot where Herr Fleischmann walks away from the group of people and approaches a tree, feeling its shape by gently touching—almost embracing—the branches, is unforgettable; it's an entire human drama played out in two minutes, and one of the

---

[48]Ibid., p. 501.

deepest moments audiences will ever encounter in a film. If you were to show that scene to someone who hadn't seen the whole film, it would seem insignificant. What's happening on screen at that moment is startlingly simple, and anyone who tuned into the film would think, "It's just a shot of a man touching a tree." But this is an image that requires the preceding one and a half hours for audiences to be sufficiently receptive to its power. … The inner rhythm inexorably leads us to the final sequence, and as soon as I saw Herr Fleischmann under that tree I knew I had the last scene of the film. It was one of those things that occasionally fall into my lap and that I wonder if I really deserve. (Cronin, 85–6)

The sequence summarizes the whole film and much of Herzog's interest in unusual achievements of selfhood. Prepared by the film's prior investigations of tactile forms of consciousness and experience among the deaf-blind, we visually explore an extended image of a man tactilely exploring his distinctive world, with his experience acting as a metaphor for our viewing experience and vice versa. Moving experiences with distinct phenomenologies are possible, these reciprocal metaphors tell us, and having them and paying attention to them is central to sustaining selfhood.

In the voice-over narration to *The Great Ecstasy of the Woodcarver Steiner* (1973), a movie that follows the Swiss ski-jumping champion Walter Steiner, Herzog tell us that "to be like him is still my dream today." As opposed to going through the motions of ordinary life without distinct feeling or commitment, for Herzog "ski-jumping is not only something athletic, but rather a mind set, i.e. how has one already overcome death. It is a question of solitude, of surrendering oneself to the utmost imaginable still remaining for a human being."[49]

---

[49]Herzog, Gregor, Hohlweg, and Jansen, eds, *Herzog/Kluge/Straub*, p. 130; cited in English in Koch, "Blindness as Insight," p. 78.

At the beginning of the film, after an initial shot of Steiner ski-jumping and then the opening credits, we see Steiner in his workshop, describing a gnarled log on which he is working. "For instance, I saw this bowl here and the way the shape recedes: it's as if an explosion had happened and the force cannot escape properly and is caught up everywhere. Here you can see how everything is caught up, and all the energy and yet it's full of tension." The evident issue here is whether, and, if so, how energies trapped within the human subject can be released so as to achieve fuller and more authentic selfhood.

For Steiner, this release—his ecstasy—comes in ski-flying, that is, ski-jumping on very large hills. In 1973, he had jumped 179 meters, but crashed, suffering a concussion and a fractured rib. 10 meters more would have had him landing on the flat area, unable to control his speed and likely dying as a result. This jump would have been a world record, if the competition had not then been forced to move to a lower starting point. The film now follows him in a 1974 competition in Planica, Romania. On the first day of practice, Steiner flies 169 meters and ties the world record. On the second day, he jumps 179 meters from a shorter ramp, but falls during his landing, resulting in shock, confusion, and loss of memory. It becomes an issue which ramp should be used.

> I tell them something [—the start is too high up—], and they laugh at me and say I brood too much. They say there's no need [to shorten the ramp]. Things would be okay if they listened to one man, and that's me. I have a right to talk that way. But as soon as I open my mouth, they say I brood and talk rot. So I have to prove it, but proving it isn't so funny, not funny at all.

On the third day, the first day of official competition, Steiner voluntarily starts one ramp lower than the other jumpers. On the fourth day, he jumps 166 meters with a perfect landing and a perfect score.

Toward the end of the film, Steiner describes a pet raven he had had as a child. "It was a torture to see him harmed by his own kind because he couldn't fly anymore." This remark is surely meant (by Steiner and by Herzog) to be self-referential: what torture would life be, if flying (literal or metaphorical) were no longer possible? The film ends after this remark with extreme slow motion shots of Steiner in flight, until he lands and is silhouetted from a distance against nothing but empty white snow, having achieved and completed his ecstasy.

Roger Cook usefully describes Herzog's filmic technique in enabling viewers to share in Steiner's ecstasies and so to appreciate the importance of ecstasies in life.

As he presents several of Steiner's jumps throughout the course of the film, he is searching for the perfect technique that not only displays the ecstasy of flight, but also lets the viewer experience it. This requires a filmic strategy that enables the viewer to engage with the movement and force of the film rather than view it from a more distant, observational point of view. The slow-motion footage extends the duration of the flight phase, facilitating the viewer's ability to assume a state of consciousness similar to that of the ski flyer. The placement of the cameras guides perception and spatial orientation in the viewer in a way that enhances the feeling of flight. The music evokes feelings of elation similar to those experienced during dreams of flying and, presumably, during the flight phase of the jump. ... Herzog presents all of his most accomplished jumps in slow motion, focusing the attention primarily on the phase of flight. Herzog situates his cameras so as to remove the ground from sight during the flight phase of the jump and reduce the proprioceptive sense of weight normally produced through vision. The effect with respect both to the body of the ski jumper and to the virtual body of the viewing subject as it is situated via the camera is an enhanced sense of weightlessness. … Then during the second part of the jump, the camera follows him from above so that we see him descending with the slope, crowd, and rest of the surroundings as backdrop. In this way the viewer takes part in the shift from a state of suspended conscious perception during flight to awareness of the approaching surface and the need to negotiate a smooth landing.[50]

We share in Steiner's point of view and imaginatively in his feelings, as we explore the image of the distant crowd, with the

Figure 11 *Steiner in flight, from* The Great Ecstasy of the Woodcarver Steiner *(1974).*

---

[50]Roger F. Cook, "The Ironic Ecstasy of Werner Herzog: Embodied Vision in *The Great Ecstasy of Woodcarver Steiner,*" in *A Companion to Werner Herzog*, ed. Prager, pp. 281–300, at pp. 290, 291, 292.

experience framed by the minimalist-triumphant Popol Vuh soundtrack. Overtitles at the end read, "I ought to be all alone in the world, just me, Steiner, and no other living thing. No sun, no culture, myself, naked on a high rock, no storm, no snow, no banks, no money, no time, no breath. Then, at least, I wouldn't be afraid." Anxieties of reception and rejection are overcome in the ability to live and to have pure experiences on one's own. Steiner echoes Aguirre's dream of pure self-creation, but instead of collapsing into Aguirre's madness, he achieves selfhood in the momentary graces of ski-flying, just as Herzog achieves it in the graces of the filmic images that make Steiner's experiences available to us.

"Naked on a high rock" is a literal description of a central image in *Gasherbrum—The Dark Glow of the Mountains* (1984). The film follows the attempt of Reinhold Messner and his climbing partner Hans Kammerlander to climb the Himalayan peaks Gasherbrum I (8,080 meters) and Gasherbrum II (8,035 meters) near the China-Pakistan border in a single trip without returning to their base camp—a feat that had never before been accomplished. But the film is not simply a documentary record of mountain climbing. Instead, Herzog's voice-over tells us:

> We weren't particularly interested in making a film about the act of mountain climbing, or about climbing techniques. What we wanted to find out was: what goes on inside mountain climbers who undertake these extreme endeavors? What is the fascination that drives them to the peaks as though they were addicts? Aren't these mountains and peaks something akin to a characteristic deep within each of us?

This characteristic deep within each of us—often unacknowledged or suppressed—is a need to exercise human powers fully (here, as often in Herzog, in physical activity under limit conditions), impress oneself into the world, and achieve selfhood.

Reinhold Messner is well aware that pursuing this need in mountain climbing is not the stuff of ordinary life.

> I don't have a normal profession. I never learned one thing that I can say I mastered. I've done a lot of things. I can make a living doing many things. That's all I need. I can finance my expeditions by selling mountain-climbing gear, by products. I don't need anything else. I'm very glad today that I don't have a profession. I think having a profession means the end of any kind of creative activity.

Whether or not Messner (or Herzog) is right that more ordinary or professional life makes creative activity impossible, the need for creative activity in order to feel one's life to be one's own—something actively lived rather than passively suffered—is genuine. In order to pursue this genuine need, something other than or in addition to routine is necessary (even if routine and technique are also important). Without testing oneself at the limits of technique, where judgment, imagination, and commitment are needed, one may fall into passivity and drift. Messner tells Herzog, in a thought that the film evidently endorses:

> I think all artists, all creative types, are crazy. I think I am also crazy. Art and creative activity are also forms of decadence. Nonetheless, I need, at least one a year or twice a year this possibility—[*das Maß zu finden*: to take one's measure]. There is no better possibility for a man in general to find his balance [*sein Maß zu finden*] than in climbing big mountains.

Herzog asks Messner directly what the point of climbing is, as Messner is sitting naked at the edge of glacial pool in which he has just bathed.

WH: Reinhold, you're sitting here completely naked and unprotected in front of us. I would like to ask you a completely simple question. What was the point of it all?

RM: I don't know. Just as with other crazy things I've done, I've never asked first the question about justification, about why I do it. I wouldn't like to know the answer. I myself, however, have the feeling that I can draw on these great walls, these three-four thousand meter high walls, just as a teacher draws and writes on a blackboard with chalk. On these great walls I not only write lines, imaginary lines; rather, I live these lines. I also have the feeling that afterwards these lines are there, even if I am the only one who can feel them and see them, because I lived them and survived them, and that others will never be able to see them. They are there and remain there; they will remain there for all time.

"That I have lived them"—written them actively on the walls of the mountains—is an image of fuller, less passive life and selfhood.

Dieter Dengler in *Little Dieter Needs to Fly* (1997) is the most unambiguous and cheerful hero in Herzog's oeuvre. Part of his unassuming charm is that he disclaims being a hero, despite his Distinguished Flying Cross, Navy Cross, Purple Heart, and other military medals. "I'm not a hero … Only dead people are heroes." Like the ski-jumper Walter Steiner (and like Graham Dorrington in *The White Diamond* [2004]), for Dieter (and for Herzog) flying is an embodiment of freedom. Dieter traces his dream of flying to a fairly close sight of a US Air Force pilot in his cockpit, strafing his house in the Black Forest during the Second World War. After presenting Dieter as he lives today, followed by an account of his childhood and then training in the United States to become a Navy pilot, the bulk of the film consists of documentary shots and reenactments of Dieter's escape from his Pathet Lao and North Vietnamese captors, after he had been shot down over Laos. "Play along with them [Thais now standing in as Dieter's re-enactment captors]. Running like this might chase the demons away," Herzog instructs him. Visually, it is less striking than most other Herzog films, perhaps in part because Herzog's own attitude toward Dieter is so thoroughly positive: shaped by both Dieter's current personality and the actual, documented events of his life in surviving capture and torture. "Being with Dieter was a constant joy," Herzog reports; "he had such an intense enjoyment of life. ... [He] was a unique man with extraordinary survival instincts, alongside great integrity and pride, and wasn't affected by his experiences as much as most other people would have been" (Cronin, 315, 317). Herzog regards him as "a quintessential immigrant who came to America not just to find a job, but as a man with a big dream. ... He possessed all the qualities that make America so wonderful: self-reliance and courage, a readiness to take risks, a kind of frontier spirit" (Cronin, 318), qualities that Herzog might claim for himself as an American immigrant as well. Dieter "emerged from his experiences without so much as a hint of bitterness; he was forever able to bear the misery [of his captivity and desperately arduous escape] with great optimism" (Cronin, 319). Dieter's bearing throughout the film consistently confirms this judgment of his character, despite "the nightmares he had immediately after his rescue" (Cronin, 320). The final shots of the film show Dieter visiting Davis-Monthan Air Force base outside Tucson, Arizona, the so-called boneyard for leftover US military aircraft. With the celebratory Malagasy song "Oay Lahy É" ["O! Dear Friend"] on the soundtrack, we see Dieter walking amid the tens of thousands of planes, as he utters the line (scripted by Herzog [Cronin, 321]), "One could really feel at home here. It's just a heaven for pilots."

Figure 12 *Dieter in the aircraft boneyard: "It's just a heaven for pilots," from* Little Dieter Needs to Fly *(1997).*

"And thus Little Dieter got it all," the overtitles tell us, "from horizon to horizon the planet covered with aircraft against the anguish of the night." The credits roll over an orchestral version of Bartok's wistful, elegiac Romanian folk dance "Buciumeana," music that had also opened the movie. A 2001 Postscript shows Dieter's Arlington National Cemetery funeral with full military honors, including a military band and a flyover by F14s.

Wings of Hope (Julianes Sturz in den Dschungel) (2000) is a close companion piece to *Little Dieter*. Both were made for German television; both recount plane crashes and subsequent escapes from the jungle. Juliane Koepcke is a German mammalian biologist who, as a seventeen-year-old, having just completed high school in Lima, Peru, boarded a flight along with her mother on Christmas Eve, 1971, from Lima to Pucallpa, Peru in the Amazonian jungle, in order to join her father who ran an ecological research station there. As it happens, Herzog had been scheduled to be on the very same flight, but had been prevented from taking it by repair trouble and overbooking. The plane crashed in the jungle with Juliane as the only survivor. Like *Little Dieter, Wings of Hope* uses reenactments to present Juliane's twelve-day trek out of the jungle. Here too Herzog's attitude is positive. "Juliane is rather straight-talking and clear-headed. The only reason she survived her ordeal was because of her ability to act methodically in the face of such dire circumstances" (Cronin, 325). Despite her competence, clear-headedness, and maturity, there is nonetheless some suggestion that mastering her experience has been some work for her. The film opens with a shot of Juliane walking through a city street of shops featuring mannequins with distorted faces, with Herzog's voice-over narration:

> In her dreams Juliane often sees herself on the streets of a city—shops, display windows, bargains; everything seems normal. And then all of a sudden the faces she encounters are broken, the heads all smashed, disfigured, but strangely enough she's not afraid. ... And yet Juliane seemed to be emotionally untouched by all of this. This shell, she later said, was a necessary protective device, part of a technique she developed to lead a somewhat normal life. ... Juliane has her safeguards against the horror. She has frequent dreams about shelves, cases, and racks where millions of butterflies are stored away—all existing species of this world. It is, she says, as if I could safely lock away all the airplanes in the world so that they could not hurt me anymore.

The bulk of the film then follows Juliane as she returns with Herzog to the crash site, where she recounts her experiences of both the crash and her trek out of the jungle and back into contact with other people. We learn of her broken collarbone, her feelings at the loss of her mother, the maggots in the wound in her shoulder, and her strategy in following small rivers downstream in order to find settlements. The most striking visual sequence occurs, as is often the case in Herzog, at the end of the film. For the final 3:21 seconds, with the Prelude to Wagner's *Das Rheingold*—music of entry into another world—on the soundtrack, Herzog narrates Juliane's thoughts as she finds herself "months later, released from a hospital, ... in an airplane again." Present-tense footage of Juliane at various sites of her trek is intercut with past-tense photos, staged reenactments by actors, and present-tense shots of workers shifting about fragments of the plane. Herzog's voice-over tells us that:

> She wants to reassemble the whole thing [the plane], but it dawns on her that nothing can be reversed, nothing can be annulled. ... Alone, strapped to her seat, she sails on further and further. Around her there's nothing but a yawning abyss. She flies on for weeks. Then it becomes dark. As it becomes bright again, she sees a way out, a door of deliverance. She walks through the door. All of a sudden she beholds an angel engulfed in light. All fear departs from her. All screaming falls silent. She doesn't breathe anymore. Overwhelmed by bliss, her heart stands still for an entire minute, and she knows that a boat will come slowly and softly to carry her away, to rescue her at last.

What seems to be at stake here is a general account, presented through the figure of Juliane, of what it would be fully to acknowledge one's finite life in time ("nothing can be reversed, nothing can be annulled"), as it is marked both by catastrophe and by possibilities of rescue and bliss. These latter possibilities are present, but perhaps only realizable with the help of good character, luck, and the unforeseen interventions of others, not by following any straightforward script of achievement. Character, fortune, and responsiveness to circumstances fraught with danger are more important than belief or doctrine.

"It's all about confronting chaos, impending chaos," Graham Dorrington, the central figure of *The White Diamond* (2004), tells us. Dorrington is a British aeronautical engineer who designs small, two-person airships to float over the top of the Amazonian jungle canopy in Guyana, in order to search for medicinal plants. His life has, in fact, been marked by accidents: the loss of two fingers at age fourteen in a model rocket explosion, tangled valves and electrical wires in his current airship—"ropes never untangle themselves; they tangle up. They become complex with time. Because human beings want them to be untangled. Maybe that's our mistake. We try and impose order on the chaos of the universe"—a reversed electrical motor that prevents proper forward progress and steering, a broken propeller, and, most importantly, the accidental death of the photographer Dieter Plage on a prior expedition in Sumatra. (Plage fell from a single-person airship while filming. In his full account of the accident, Dorrington reports that Dieter's body "hit the ground with a thud ... like meat in a butcher shop.") In the face of chaos, accidents, and death, Dorrington (like Steiner and Dieter) dreams of flying as both a central form of and a striking metaphor for meaningful motion through life.

> We can realize our dreams. That's, that's the thing I've learned this whole project is that you start from a concept, you do the design, and you can actually see your ideas being made, and you can realize dreams. It's just a simple step, and it just requires a little bit of determination. But you can do it; you can do it—whatever you want. You just have to have that dream, and just, and then just zoom up: that's the thing. Let's go fly! Let's go fly!

Herzog's voice-over narration adds that "the age old dream of flying was realized in the late 18th century like a fever dream of the mechanical age."

What flying above all makes possible for Dorrington is escape from chaos and noise, into calm and a sense of meaningfulness.

> With all the motors off. It would lovely just to be above the canopy in complete silence. I just think that, it's today, have you not noticed that there are so many aircraft; everything is so noisy. And when you get a bit of peace and quiet—just quiet—then you have a chance to think … just quietly floating above the forest, in those mists.

In counterpoint to Dorrington there are surrounding expedition porters, mine workers, a young man who break dances above Kaieteur Falls, and, especially Mark Anthony Yhap, a man of all jobs who would like to take his rooster, Red Man, on a balloon flight with him. (Roger Ebert remarks in his review of the film that "there are times when this expedition causes us to speculate that the Monty Python troupe might have based its material on close observation of actual living Britons."[51]) Yhap is suffused with wonder toward the phenomena of life. "My rooster means so much to me. He's such a lovely guy." He rhapsodizes, with serene calm and humor, over the beauty of the balloon, the variety of animal life in the rain forest, and the waterfall. Yhap's open wonder balances Dorrington's obsessive eccentricity and inventiveness. In different ways, they are each open to perceptual experiences of astonishment and admiration at the unfolding of the world in time, and it is the two of them, in conversation on a rock ledge at the edge of Kaieteur Falls, who introduce the extraordinary final footage of the swifts circling the falls.[52]

---

[51] Ebert, *Herzog by Ebert*, p. 76.
[52] See Chapter 2 on Nature for an extended description and analysis of this sequence.

Like, in their various ways, Huie Rogers, Gene Scott, Walter Steiner, Reinhold Messner, Fini Staubinger, Dieter Dengler, Juliane Koepcke, and Graham Dorrington, Timothy Treadwell (*Grizzly Man*, [2005]) is for Herzog a figure of self-invention and the achievement of selfhood, outside the bounds of the ordinary. "It was as if he had become a star by virtue of his own invention," Herzog's narration tells us. He "crossed an invisible borderline" to produce "a film of ecstasies and darkest inner turmoil." Treadwell becomes, according to Herzog, the subject of investigation of his own films, as much as or more so than the bears themselves. "The camera was his only present companion. It was his instrument to explore the wilderness around him, but increasingly it became something more. He started to scrutinize his innermost being, his demons, his exhilarations. Facing the lens of a camera took on the quality of a confessional."

This exploration of possibilities of selfhood within one's own character, in extreme circumstances, by way of the use of the camera makes Treadwell a director figure with whom Herzog clearly identifies.

I have seen this madness [in Treadwell's footage] on a movie set before. … I have seen human ecstasies and darkest human turmoil. … Having myself filmed in the wilderness of jungles, I found that beyond the wildlife film in his material lay dormant a story with astonishing beauty and depth. I discovered a film of human ecstasies and darkest inner turmoil. As if there was a desire in him to leave the confinements of his humanness, Treadwell reached out, seeking a primordial encounter.

Here a primordial encounter is an encounter that takes place outside the framework of ordinary, settled, commercial life and business as usual. It is something that has the potential to confer a sense of meaning within one's bearing throughout this encounter, and in virtue of having that potential it is something that we need in modern life, in

Herzog's judgment. A central ambition of his films is to discover such experiences on the parts of others, to track their developments, and to make analogues of them perceptually available to viewers. In the director's commentary to *Encounters at the End of the World* (2007), Herzog describes the film as about "individuals who fell in love with the world"—a suitable description of Herzog's ambitions for himself and for those who view his work aptly. Herzog ends *Into the Abyss* (2011), a film about three pointless, gruesome murders committed by two nineteen-year-old boys and about the death penalty, with the testimony of Fred Allen, who has suddenly retired as captain of the prison execution squad, as he finds himself unable to do the work any longer, after having presided over the 1998 execution of Karla Fay Tucker, the first woman executed in Texas since 1863. Describing his experiences and his current thinking about capital punishment, Allen tells us that he is resolved now to "live the dash": the period of time between the dates of birth and death that will appear on one's tombstone.

> Hold still and watch the birds. And you know, once you get up into your life like that, and once you feel good about your life, you under- ... you do start watching what the birds do, you know, what the ducks are doing, like, the hummingbirds. Wow, there's so many of them.

This is, for Allen, something he had failed to do during his prison career as an executioner, and it is evidently according to Herzog something many or most of us fail to do for much of our lives, as we fail to "get up into your life like that."

In this thought about the stultifying and gray character of modern industrial-commercial life, and in the further thought that we might somehow do better otherwise, especially if nurtured by intense perceptual experiences rather than stale, abstract doctrines, Herzog joins company with core modernist writers such as Kierkegaard, Rilke, Joyce, and Woolf. Hegel describes the achievement of selfhood—one's distinctively human powers meaningfully realized within courses of action, in ways that others can endorse—as a matter of bringing one's self-certainty to truth.[53] One begins with an initially inchoate sense of who one is and how one might specifically actualize one's human and personal powers. Over time, this sense becomes both more articulate and more accurate to what one in fact does, as one forms oneself to exercise important skills through training, apprenticeship, and education. For Hegel, success in this enterprise is significantly, even centrally, a matter of becoming a "citizen of a state with good laws."[54] Whatever the pertinence of this thought in stating a possible condition for the achievement of selfhood, most of us are likely to find it insufficient and, often enough, unavailable. For most of us, and for Herzog, it does not suffice for the achievement of selfhood simply to be well brought up within the way things are mostly done. Courage, openness to perceptual and aesthetic experience, and risk will all be necessary. In a speech given in Milan after a showing of *Lessons of Darkness*, Herzog endorses Longinus's "concept of *ekstasis*, a person's stepping out of himself into an elevated state—where we can raise ourselves over our own nature. … Here I am taking the liberty to apply that notion to rare and fleeting moments in film."[55] However difficult the achievement

[53]See G. W. F. Hegel, *Phenomenology of Spirit*, trans. A. V. Miller (Oxford: Clarendon Press, 1977), 166-7, pp. 104-5, 394-5, pp. 236-7.

[54]Hegel, *Elements of the Philosophy of Right*, trans. H. B. Nisbet, ed. Allen W. Wood (Cambridge: Cambridge University Press, 1991), §153R, p. 196.

[55]Werner Herzog, "On the Absolute, the Sublime, and Ecstatic Truth," trans. Moira Weigel, *Arion* 17, 3 (2010), p. 8.

of at least some measure of fuller selfhood may be, it is not altogether impossible, as the examples of Herzog's various central figures show, in their circumscribed successes and ecstasies, their characters, and their defeats by the social circumstances those defeats indict, and as his films themselves directly intimate to us in their own perceptual sublimities. "Guerilla tactics are best. … Get used to the bear behind you."

4

History

I'm fascinated by the notion of civilization as a thin layer of ice resting upon a deep ocean of darkness and chaos.

—WERNER HERZOG (CRONIN, 5)

Herzog's career has frequently been shadowed by public controversies about the representation of historical events and, more broadly, his treatments of non-Europeans, both during filming and within individual films. *Ballad of the Little Soldier* (1984)—a film about the use and the experiences of child soldiers among the Miskito Indian resistance to the Sandinista government of Nicaragua—was widely criticized by the Left for seeming to accuse the Sandinistas of genocide. The activist-historian Roxanne Dunbar Ortiz, who worked with and wrote professionally about the Miskito, distributed leaflets at San Francisco showings of the film that labeled Herzog "an opportunistic lackey for the CIA."[1] In a letter about the film, Herzog writes, "I hesitate to say too much about politics, about history, about ideology, about spheres of power, and zones of influence. My film is not a film against the Sandinistas, or anyone; it is a film with and for

---

[1]George Paul Csicsery, "*Ballad of the Little Soldier*: Werner Herzog in a Political Hall of Mirrors," *Film Quarterly* 39, 2 (Winter 1985–86), pp. 7–15, at p. 7.

the Miskitos, and they have a voice in it."[2] To some viewers, however, it is the very effort to avoid the political situation—what George Paul Csicsery calls Herzog's "metapolitical stance"[3]—that is the heart of the problem.

The same metapolitical stance is at the heart of Herzog's 1992 *Lessons of Darkness*, a film that is nominally about the first Gulf War (August 1990–February 1991), but that fails to present any information about who invaded whom when, or who caused which casualties and damage where and when, preferring instead to present raging oil fires and efforts to extinguish them as moments within the progress of a decontextualized apocalypse. At the Berlin Film Festival, Herzog reports that:

> Nearly two thousand people rose up with a single voice in an angry roar. They accused me of "aestheticising" the horror, and so hated the film that when I walked down the aisle after the screening people spat at me. I was told that *Lessons of Darkness* was dangerously authoritarian, and so—finding all this hostility rather invigorating—I decided to be authoritarian at my very best. I stood before them and said, "Mr. Dante did the same thing in his inferno, and Mr. Goya did it in his paintings. Brueghel and Bosch too. You cretins are all wrong." (Cronin, 293)

This neither endeared him to his audience nor established the credibility of his political stance. "You should have heard the tornado of disgust" (Cronin, 293) at his remarks, Herzog tells us. He then adds that:

---

[2] Herzog, Letter to George Csicsery, 6/85, cited in ibid., p. 15.
[3] Ibid.

War has no fascination for me beyond its absurdity and insanity, and *Lessons of Darkness* consciously transcends the topical and the particular; this could be any war and any country. The film is about the evil that human beings are capable of, which is why it will never age. It is precisely because Iraq and Kuwait aren't named that humanity will always respond to these sounds and images. (Cronin, 294)

Plausible as this remark may be—the images are compelling— it does little to rebut the charges of aestheticization and the adoption of a metapolitical stance involving lack of interest in issues of responsibility and blame.

The making of *Fitzcarraldo* (1982) became caught up in a border war between Peru and Ecuador (Cronin, 182), and Herzog was accused of "torturing and imprisoning Native Indians" (Cronin, 195) during shooting. Herzog dismisses this accusation as "bizarre" (Cronin, 195), and there has never been any evidence to support it. Nonetheless, controversy about the making of the film lingers. In the Les Blank documentary *Burden of Dreams* (1982) about the making of *Fitzcarraldo*, an engineer reports that there is a "70 percent chance of catastrophe" attaching to the effort to haul a 320-ton steamship over a mountain, using ropes alone: the giant ropes may break and fly lethally into surrounding Indian workers, or the suddenly untethered, sliding ship may crush them. In fact, substantial precautions were taken, nothing happened, and the ship was successfully moved; nonetheless, in some quarters suspicions about Herzog's practices and attitudes have lingered.

Criticisms about the avoidance of the representation of historical and political realities have also been directed at Herzog's fiction films. Will Lehman charges that "in his early Amazonian films [*Aguirre, Fitzcarraldo*] Herzog was reluctant to re-inscribe Hollywood conventions and popular German expectations of Indians, focusing instead on the European as a spectacle against the backdrop of the jungle, rather than featuring Indians in their native and domestic spaces."[4] That is, although not determined by the conventions of Hollywood or by German Karl May conceptions of Indians, Europeans and spectacle are nonetheless foregrounded over how Native American peoples actually live. Lehman also finds this tendency toward nonrepresentation of Native American Indians in Herzog's later documentary films. "In later films [*Ten Thousand Years Older, Ballad of the Little Soldier*], however, Indians are increasingly highlighted as performers within the *mise-en-scène* of the jungle. But rather than staging some kind of native authenticity, these performers appear as players in anachronistic epilogues of dramas in which they and their cultures have already died, swept into the abyss of modernity."[5]

Roger Hillman similarly finds an erasure of history and accurate representation in the documentaries, specifically achieved by Herzog's uses of mythico-religious musical soundtracks instead of recording the actual sounds and speech that accompany the actions he films. In *Pilgrimage* (2001) in particular, Hillman charges:

> The lack of ambient sound effaces what cultural anthropologist David Tomas calls "ephemeral and fragmentary histories." When dialogue is also absent, what remains creates the parameters for sonic myth, an acoustic equivalent of the oneiric state traditionally associated with Herzog's images as rendered by his cinematography. Whatever the degree of empathy established with the devotees in

[4]Will Lehman, "A March into Nothingness: The Changing Course of Herzog's Indian Images," in *A Companion to Werner Herzog*, ed. Prager (Oxford: Wiley-Blackwell, 2012), pp. 371–92, at p. 390.
[5]Ibid.

the film *Pilgrimage*, they are never represented from within. ...
Music is used here to immunize the viewer against anything other
than the ecstatic truth.[6]

Finally, and most pointedly, Eric Rentschler finds in Herzog's pursuit
of ecstatic truth in *Heart of Glass* (1976) nothing less than the
reactionary reincarnation of the aestheticized politics of spectacle of
Nazi Germany.

> *Heart of Glass* for all its apparent elusiveness and seeming hypnotic
> appeal, operates along lines akin to what Jeffrey Herf has termed
> "reactionary modernism." It blends the rhetoric of nature and an
> embrace of the elemental characteristic of the romantic legacy
> with a forward-looking enthusiasm, a hope for a new order
> bringing purification and relief, a discourse quite prominent
> among conservative German intellectuals, poets, engineers, and
> politicians during the Weimar Republic and the Third Reich.[7]

These charges are more or less immediately plausible. Herzog is
interested in ecstatic truth disclosed by way of aesthetic images, and
the images *are* aesthetically overwhelming. His interests in filmmaking
are on the whole more existential, ontological, and transfigurationally
normative than they are descriptive, sociohistorical, and oriented
toward local political problems. It should be noted, however, that
Herzog has sometimes made films with more immediately political,
topical subject matter: *The Flying Doctors of East Africa* (1969) on the
work of the African Medical and Research Foundation in Tanzania

---

[6]Roger Hillman, "The Viewer and Herzog's Sonic Worlds," in *A Companion to Werner Herzog*, ed. Prager, pp. 168–86, at p. 179, citing David Tomas, *Transcultural Space and Transcultural Beings* (Boulder: Westview Press, 1996), p. 105.

[7]Eric Rentschler, "The Politics of Vision: Herzog's *Heart of Glass*," in *The Films of Werner Herzog*, ed. Corrigan (London: Routledge, 1986), pp. 159–81, at p. 174.

and Kenya, *Into the Abyss* (2011) on capital punishment, and *From One Second to the Next* (2013) on the perils of texting while driving. These are, however, among his most report-like, least stylized works, so that they are furthest from his signature style and concerns. On the whole, Herzog sees himself more as a Jeremiah-like prophet-poet critic than as someone who is directly intervening in local political problems. In *Self-Portrait* (1986), Herzog presents himself visually as striding across the misty Bavarian mountains, wearing heavy boots and a cape, in a way that analogizes him to the poet-prophet Hias in *Heart of Glass*. His stance in filmmaking is closer to Nietzsche's remark that "we are unknown to ourselves, we knowers: and with good reason. We have never looked for ourselves,—so how are we ever supposed to *find* ourselves?"[8] than it is to any directly documentary-political intention. We stand in need of finding ourselves—of a radical reorientation of our thoughts, feelings, perceptions, and interests— rather than in need of more piecemeal reforms within accepted frameworks of orientation and concern.

Even if specific, institutional political issues are largely absent from Herzog's work, however, it does not follow that there is no concern with politics or history in it. In a 1968 article, Herzog explicitly accepts the impossibility of neutrality and the unavoidability of politics in filmmaking.

A filmmaker cannot and must not keep his films out of the political debate. For such a standpoint, the situation in the field of cultural politics has become far too serious. In these times of upheaval it is no longer possible to try and rescue one's film and shelter it in the safe corner of neutrality. A filmmaker can no longer remain neutral,

---

[8]Friedrich Nietzsche, *On the Genealogy of Morals*, ed. Keith Ansell-Pearson, trans. Carol Diethe, 2nd ed. (Cambridge: Cambridge University Press, 2006), p. 3.

nor can he make the excuse that it is really everybody else who has turned his film into a political statement. … The politicizing of film, however, is fraught with dangers. This is to say that as soon as a crucial political moment is reached, what is expected of a film is automatically reduced. Film can no longer develop its full potential with regard to content and style, because everybody's interest will be focused on some palpable results to be gleaned from it. Instead of gaining an awareness of issues and developing questions, people will—according to the film's political stance—primarily read or even force arguments out of it.[9]

The issue then is not the absence of politics in Herzog's films, but rather what sorts of unusual political concerns—ones that challenge the ready to hand commitments of political critic-journalists occupied with immediate issues; ones that refuse "palpable results to be gleaned" from them—are present in them essentially by way of stylization. As is already evident in his consistent treatment of the fragility of human life within the chaos of nature, Herzog is worried about anarchy, barbarism, and a possible collapse of human civilization as such, and he is worried that the forms of political and cultural organization in which anyone might take pride might be nothing other than vehicles of barbarism. These worries come to the fore in his remarks about his 1961 visit to the Democratic Republic of the Congo at the age of nineteen. Civilization as such, and especially German civilization, may have barbarism at its very heart.

Congo had just won its independence and the deepest anarchy and darkest violence immediately set in. Every trace of civilization

---

[9]Herzog, "Mit den Wölfen Heulen," *Filmstudio* 1968, trans. Martina Lauster, in Paul Cronin, "Visionary Vehemence: Ten Thoughts about Werner Herzog," in *Werner Herzog—A Guide for the Perplexed* (New York: Farrar, Straus, and Geroux, 2014), p. xxix.

disappeared, every form of organization and security was gone, and there was a return to tribalism and cannibalism. I'm fascinated by the notion of civilization as a thin layer of ice resting upon a deep ocean of darkness and chaos, and by observing Africa hoped to better understand the origins of Nazism in Germany, how it could have happened that the country lost every trace of civilisation in the course of only a few years. To all appearances Germany was a civilized, stable nation, with a great tradition in many fields— philosophy, mathematics, literature and music—when suddenly, during the era of the Third Reich, everything overwhelmingly dangerous in the country was brought out into the open. Strange that at the centre of Europe is a nation that, deep in its heart, is still barbarian. (Cronin, 5)

Thematically, worries about barbarism, and especially European barbarism, are at the center of a significant number of Herzog's fiction films, especially *Aguirre* (1972), *Where the Green Ants Dream* (1984), and *Invincible* (2001), which treat the violent suppression of non-dominant European ways of life. *Even Dwarfs Started Small* (1970), *Kaspar Hauser* (1974), *Stroszek* (1976), and *Woyzeck* (1979) each trace the costs that central institutions within organized, modern, industrial-commercial societies—training institutions, medical institutes, banks, police, and armies—inflict on their most vulnerable members. As Dana Benelli characterizes the main course of action of *Aguirre*, "the expedition, Spanish civilization's organized attempt to deal with the (extensive) margins of their world and subordinate its value (El Dorado) to their needs, subsequently fails, grinds to a halt and, at least figuratively, dies,"[10] therein revealing itself as a form of

---

[10]Dana Benelli, "The Cosmos and Its Discontents," in *The Films of Werner Herzog*, ed. Corrigan (1986), p. 97.

barbarism, albeit one that is ultimately impotent in the face of nature's power. In *Heart of Glass* (1976), a central idea is that settled life cannot in the end be successfully founded on knowledge. Standing in front of a display cabinet housing the ruby glass that no one any longer knows how to make, the factory owner despairingly says, "This splendor is now extinguished from the world. What will protect us now from the evil of the universe?"

Yet while criticizing Euro-American civilization in broad terms as barbaric in its treatments of both insiders and outsiders, Herzog's films deliberately offer no recipes for productive social change, perhaps in part because a tendency toward barbarism is lodged within each of us through the *ressentiment*-laden formation of the ego. In *Werner Herzog Eats His Shoe* (dir. Les Blank, 1980), Herzog responds to a question about "the value of films for society" by asking:

> Whose society? I don't know, Les. I have kept wondering ever since I have been in contact with audiences, and I have wondered what the value of films was. And I think—I don't know—it gives us some insight. It's like. It doesn't change—people have thought it would—films could cause revolutions or whatever, and it does not. But films might change our perspective of things. And ultimately, in the long term, it may be something valuable, but there's a lot of absurdity involved as well. As you see, it makes me into a clown. And that happens to everyone. … It's because what we do as filmmakers is immaterial. It's only a projection of light. And doing that all your life makes you just a clown. And it's an almost inevitable process.

Even though they are not dominated by an ameliorist or even consistently sociohistorical-documentary intention, Herzog's projections of life are overwhelmingly responsive to cultural difference, that is, to lived cultural and religio-aesthetic experiences that lie outside the orbit of advanced industrial-commercial life. In

Burden of Dreams, over shots of the faces of Campa Indian men, women, and children, Herzog tells us that:

> In this case [*Fitzcarraldo* (1982)], we will probably have one of the last feature films with authentic natives in it. They are fading away very quickly. And it's a catastrophe and a tragedy that's going on and we are losing riches and riches and riches. And we lose cultures and individualities and languages and mythologies and we'll be stark naked. At the end we'll end up like all the cites in the world now, with skyscrapers and a universal kind of culture, like the American culture. I don't feel like doing a documentary on the Campas. And it should not end up as an ethnographic film. I also stylize them, and I have them in the film as they probably are not precisely in their normal life. They do things that they normally would not do. They act in that film. And that interests me even more. Yet they have an authenticity of their culture and their behavior, their movements, their language that will just disappear from the face of the earth. I don't want to live in a world where there are no lions any more or where there are no people like lions, and they are lions.[11]

Clearly, there is something wrong, according to Herzog, with "a universal kind of culture" on the American commercial model. The image of the Campas as being "like lions" in their authenticity suggests a powerfully felt discharge of bodily energy in "their behavior, their movements, their language" that by implication contrasts with what Herzog takes to be the paleness and half-heartedness of action within modern industrial-commercial routines. Without their kind

---

[11]These remarks are also printed in *Burden of Dreams: Screenplay, Journals, Reviews, Photographs*, eds Les Blank and James Bogan (Berkeley, CA: North Atlantic Books, 1984), p. 36.

of energetic authenticity, we risk being "stark naked" in reducing ourselves to little more than fungible units of production and consumption of standardized commodities.

Herzog expresses guarded support for the idea that perception is at least sometimes significantly shaped by culture. In making *The Flying Doctors of East Africa* (1969), he reports that:

> We took … posters—one of a man, one of a human eye that filled an entire piece of paper, another of a hut—and conducted an experiment. I asked [the Masai villagers] if they could identify the human eye, and most of the villagers couldn't; the images were just abstract compositions to them. One man thought the window of the hut was an eye, and another pointed to the eye and said, "This is the rising sun." It was clear that certain elements of visual perception are in some way culturally conditioned, that these people were processing images differently to how Westerners might. (Cronin, 57)

In *The White Diamond* (2004), Herzog has Graham Dorrington first tell a scripted story about Pacific Island Maoris being unable to see Captain Cook's boats upon their first landing and then speculate that the children in the Guyanan village may have been unable to see the airship he has just flown close by them. Yet Herzog does not argue that perception is thoroughly culturally determined or even that these cases make much sense. About the Captain Cook-Maori story he says:

> It's a wonderful idea, but doesn't sound very likely. After all, the Aztecs could clearly see the Spanish fleet of Cortés, and in the *Florentine Codex* there are accurate descriptions and illustrations of a sighting of distant galleons and the landing of ships. … Human figures in ancient Egyptian art are shown only in profile, but the fact that the Egyptians didn't represent perspective doesn't mean that they couldn't recognize and understand it in real life. (Cronin, 57)

Instead of a general thesis about vision, then, Herzog's thought must be first that visual perceptions, as well as the actions that flow from them, can be sometimes either fresh or stale, natural or difficult, and second that we stand in some need of fresher, more difficult perceptions than we mostly have—perceptions that his films undertake to supply to their viewers. This thought in turn explains his consistent presentation in his documentaries of stylized, ecstatic experience on the parts of those who are not normally represented in mainstream commercial films: the Wodaabe of the African Sahel (*Wodaabe, Herdsmen of the Sun*, 1989), the Russian mystics of *Bells from the Deep* (1993), the Mexican and Russian pilgrims of *Pilgrimage* (2001), and the Buddhist pilgrims of *Wheel of Time* (2003), among others. Even if they are unavailable to us, their viewers, the ecstasies of these peoples stand as a rebuke to industrial-commercial half-heartedness.

What understanding of history is both implicit in and helps to make sense of Herzog's understanding of problems within industrial-commercial life and of his turn to visual rebuke? In Convolute N, titled "On the Theory of Knowledge, Theory of Progress," of his uncompleted *Arcades Project*, Walter Benjamin points to what he calls a "barbarism [that] lurks in the very concept of culture."[12] This barbarism consists in considering values to be "independent of the [current production process] in which they survive,"[13] as though—however they might have first been articulated—they somehow sanctify current processes of production and ways of life by being embodied in them and apt to human life as such. Value articulations so considered—stripped out of processes of production and social conflict that are always present and always changing—then function as rationalizing ideologies

[12]Walter Benjamin, *The Arcades Project*, trans. Howard Eiland and Kevin McLaughlin (Cambridge, MA: Harvard University Press, 1999), N 5a, 7, p. 467.
[13]Ibid., N 5a, 7, pp. 467–8.

that putatively justify the status quo and those who are dominant within it. In the face of the barbaric persistence of domination, within which human cultural life fails to flow meaningfully, at least for many, one must, according to Benjamin, reject business as usual and the accumulation and worship of "cultural treasures—spoils that are carried forth in a march of triumph."[14] The costs of indulging in ideological rationalization and the idolatrous worship of artifacts are "conformism," "acedia,"[15] and complacency for the lucky few and continuing domination for the many. In both cases, there is a failure to express and expend human energy in meaningful, self-actualizing activity, as joint sociocultural life remains dominated by scripted routines and social roles that are less than fulfilling.

In the face of these ills, what is necessary, according to Benjamin, is to "brush history against the grain,"[16] that is, to move out of rationalization, boredom, conformity, and domination, and somehow into more fully meaningful activity. This can be aided by historical understanding, insofar as "history is not simply a science but also and not least a form of remembrance."[17] Where a putatively scientific history might undertake to focus systematically on what everyone has always already been doing, at least implicitly (perhaps in the manner of Hegel's story about the always already present pursuit of freedom, recognition, and self-knowledge ultimately achieved within settled institutional life), in contrast history as remembrance seizes on past, singular, exemplary possibilities of the expenditure of human energy that

---

[14]Benjamin, "On the Concept of History," trans. Harry Zohn, in Benjamin, *Selected Writings*, Vol. IV, 1938–1940, eds Howard Eiland and Michael W. Jennings (Cambridge, MA: Harvard University Press, 2003), pp. 389–400, Thesis IV, p. 391.

[15]Ibid., Thesis VI, pp. 390, 391.

[16]Ibid., Thesis IV, p. 392.

[17]Benjamin, *The Arcades Project*, N 8, 1, p. 471.

might function as individual sources of present resonances. The "concept of mankind's historical progress," as Benjamin puts it, and the picture of "an infinite perfectibility of humanity" must be replaced by "a tiger's leap into the past" that can be accomplished not by simply recording what has been, but only by way of present "construction whose site is not homogeneous, empty time, but time filled by now-time."[18] One must find "a single focal point" in the past that flashes up to guide one's present energies; "the elements of the ultimate condition do not manifest themselves as formless progressive tendencies, but are deeply rooted in every present in the forms of the most endangered, excoriated, and ridiculed ideas and products of the creative mind."[19] Historical understanding as remembrance "has annihilated within itself the idea of progress. ... Its founding concept is not progress, but actualization"[20]—the uncovering of powers of meaning-making that have flashed forth in isolated shards of significant life, to which we might now resonate, even if those shards of significance were largely suppressed or forgotten in the intervening past. "It is not that what is past casts its light on what is present, or what is present its light on what is past; rather, [current] image is that wherein what has been comes together in a flash with the now to form a constellation. In other words: image is dialectics at a standstill."[21] In a moment of arrest by an image of what has been, flashing up decontextualized from all processes of continuous

---

[18]Benjamin, "On the Concept of History," Thesis XII, pp. 394–5.

[19]Benjamin, "The Life of Students," in Benjamin, *Selected Writings*, Vol. 1, 1913–26, eds Marcus Bullock and Michael W. Jennings (Cambridge, MA: Harvard University Press, 1996), pp. 37–48, at p. 37.

[20]Benjamin, *The Arcades Project*, N 2, 3, p. 460.

[21]Ibid., N 3, 1, p. 463.

historical unfolding, one can find possibilities of present, abrupt reorientation of interest and activity.

This is a constructivist-aestheticist, high modernist image of history.[22] Resources for transfigurative present orientation are to be constructed by arranging materials from the past in order to produce a punctual, monadic image that might move one abruptly into greater responsiveness to one's world and increased possibilities of more significant action now. As Alison Ross aptly puts it, Benjamin's writing is marked by "the drive to escape from forces of totalization which is a pulse one can detect almost everywhere in his otherwise heterogeneous corpus," a drive which is directed "into a concern as to where the orientation for living will come from now that the meaning context provided by tradition is lost."[23] If this understanding sometimes seems too aesthetic-modernist, too messianic-apocalyptic, and too little concerned with a politics of reform, it nonetheless also powerfully expresses needs for change and for life otherwise to which many may resonate.

Near the end of *Fata Morgana* (1971), Herzog presents an extended sequence (7:10) that seems to function as a metaphor and metonymy for much of the stream of modern life as such. In a fixed, mid-range shot, it shows a woman in profile playing an upright piano on the right and a man toward the middle left, more or less facing the camera, playing drums, singing unintelligibly into a distortion-inducing microphone, and wearing goggles. About a third of the way into the sequence, between songs, a voice-over informs us, cryptically, that "in the Golden Age man and woman live in harmony. Now, for example,

---

[22]For a more detailed account of Benjamin's image of history, see Richard Eldridge, *Images of History: Kant, Benjamin, Freedom, and the Human Subject* (Oxford: Oxford University Press, 2016), Chs 4, 5.

[23]Alison Ross, *Walter Benjamin's Concept of the Image* (London: Routledge, 2015), p. 77.

they appear before the lens of the camera, death in their eyes, a smile on their faces, a finger in the pie. Running, they train themselves harder and harder. Weightlifting, too, is rewarding. Unforgettable, however, remains a jump from the lighthouse." As the woman and man resume their playing, their actions seem largely mechanical and inexpressive—the result, perhaps, of training themselves "harder and harder" in a now that is evidently not a Golden Age. Herzog tells us about this scene that:

> We stumbled across them, including the woman on the piano and the guy with goggles playing the drums who play some of the saddest music I have ever heard. I gave him the goggles and stuck black paper over them so he couldn't see anything We shot that scene in a brothel in Lanzarote during production on *Even Dwarfs Started Small*; she's actually the madam and he's a pimp. He was in charge of discipline and would beat any prostitute who hadn't pleased her client. In some way the film is about ruined people in ruined places, and that sequence spoke of a terrible sadness and despair. (Cronin, 63)

A similarly cryptic image of modern life as cheerless, lonely, empty, and wasted occurs in *Of Walking in Ice*, Herzog's memoir of his walk from Munich to Paris to "save" Lotte Eisner from death. "The town is awful, quite a lot of industry, cheerless Turks, just one telephone booth. Very pronounced loneliness, also. The little one must be lying in bed by now, clinging to the edge of his blanket. Today, I'm told, they're already showing the film at the Leopold; I do not dare to believe in justice."[24] As in Benjamin's perception of much of industrial-commercial modernity, these images present the opposites

---

[24]Werner Herzog, *Of Walking in Ice*, trans. Martje Herzog and Alan Greenberg (Minneapolis, MN: University of Minnesota Press, 2015), p. 35.

Figure 13 *The pimp and madam play drums and piano in the bordello, from* Fata Morgana *(1971).*

of progress and the achievement of meaningful being in the world. And as in Benjamin, if there are alternatives to a predominant drift into circumstances of despair and empty repetition, they are to be found not through a politics of reform, but rather in the punctual ecstatic ski-jumps of Walter Steiner, mountain-climbings of Reinhold Messner, or bravura sermonizings of Huie Rogers and Gene Scott. "Thwart institutional cowardice" and "Take your fate into your own hands" are two of Herzog's twenty-four pieces of advice that appear on the back dust jacket of *Werner Herzog: A Guide for the Perplexed*.

Alternatively, there are collective possibilities of resistance to modern emptiness, cheerlessness, business, and narcissism embodied within the ways of life of marginalized and threatened cultures. In the voice-over narration to *Ballad of the Little Soldier* (1984), Herzog says (misleadingly, but in order to indicate the possibility and importance of resistance), "The Indians have no illusions. They know they will always have to defend themselves, regardless of who succeeds the Sandinistas. What is of historical importance is that, for the first time since the Spanish conquest of Latin America, an Indian tribe has taken to armed resistance." Beyond armed struggle, there are further possibilities of resistance within these marginalized forms of life. Eric Ames finds in *The Lord and the Laden* (1999) "creative, resistant subjects who adopt and modify selected aspects of Catholicism for the local purpose of preserving Mayan tradition."[25] The cult of the cigar-smoking ranchero St. Simón/Maximón, the cleansing rituals, and the syncretic religious processions present "a view of post-Conquest religious performance as unorthodox and rebellious. ... New syncretic forms of religious practice and cultural expression [promote] the persistence of native identity and memory in the face of overwhelming European power."[26]

There are even minor resistances within the authentic feelings of loss, frustration, and incomprehension present in figures such as Kaspar Hauser (*The Enigma of Kaspar Hauser*, 1974) and Stroszek (*Stroszek*, 1976) or in the eccentricities of Graham Dorrington and Mark Anthony Yhap (*The White Diamond*, 2004). In *Werner Herzog Eats His Shoe* (dir. Les Blank, 1980), Herzog praises Errol Morris's film *Gates of Heaven* (1978) for its ability to present the psychic and emotional lives of its principal characters, as those lives are both shaped and inhibited by their surrounding American culture.

You don't know where the United States are standing after a State of the Union address, but after seeing that film, you will know. [It's not a film on pet cemeteries.] It's a film on a family behind all that

---

[25]Eric Ames, *Ferocious Reality: Documentary According to Werner Herzog* (Minneapolis, MN: University of Minnesota Press, 2012), p. 140.
[26]Ibid., pp. 134, 139.

with all their failures and all their dreams, and all their dramas involved. And it's the only authentic film on love and emotions and late capitalism, and maybe it's the only authentic film on loss of emotions and loss of, or distortion of feelings and degeneration of feelings. It's a very, very sad film, and very purely done. It's an extremely pure film, a very mature film. This guy came there and he did a film, his very first film, and it's a film of a very mature filmmaker.

Herzog's most direct—perhaps too direct—indictment of the ills of modern industrial-commercial life is *Where the Green Ants Dream* (1984). He tells us explicitly that the film "does represent my thoughts and disquiet about contemporary society," even if it "has a slightly self-righteous tone to it" (Cronin, 262). It was inspired in part by the travel writer Bruce Chatwin's work on dreamsongs (songs Aboriginals sing while traversing the Australian outback landscape that function as continuously unfolding means of geographic orientation) and dreamtime (a trancelike state in which the dreamer is freed from local space and time in order to enter into an eternal present, including communion with the dead). It is no accident that the film was written and shot during Herzog's mother's final illness and that it is dedicated to her memory. The film opens with shots (filmed in Kansas) of tornadoes moving across barren fields, "blurred, strange images that somehow represent the collapse of the world, even if they have nothing directly to do with the story" (Cronin, 262).

Thematically, *Where the Green Ants Dream* argues that the costs of civilization are too high, compared with the experiences of communion that are available to Aborigines. Herzog shared with Chatwin, he tells us, "the conviction that mankind's problems started the moment humans abandoned a nomadic existence, became sedentary, and began building permanent settlements" (Cronin, 257).

Within the film, the dropout anthropologist Arnold tells the principal character, the mining engineer Lance Hackett, "You better get out of here. Go back where you came from. Your civilization destroys everything, including itself." Later on, the Aboriginal elder Miliritbi tells Hackett "You white men are lost. You don't understand the land. Too many silly questions. Your presence on this earth will come to an end. You have no sense. No purpose. No direction."

The plot treats the resistance of a small Aboriginal tribe, with Miliritbi as their chief spokesman, to the mining company's efforts to test the subsoil of their land for uranium deposits. Ferguson, the chief representative for the mining company, offers compensations (cash, a percentage of the profits, an Aboriginal art center) that the Aboriginals refuse. "Are you Christian? … What would you do if I bring a bulldozer and dig up your church?," Miliritbi asks Hackett. The case ends up in the Australian Supreme Court, where the issue is, "Do plaintiffs [the Aborigines] hold in common law a lands right title prior to 1788"—the date of the arrival of the first British ships in Sydney? At the trial, Miliritbi says that he and his fellow elders have come to court in order to "prove what the land is belong and belong to the land is." When they present a sacred object as evidence of their ties to the land, the judge orders the court clerk to record it as "wooden object carved, with markings, the markings indecipherable, the significance of the markings not plain to this court," thus echoing the failures of authorities to understand marginal figures in *Kaspar Hauser* and *Woyzeck*. The judge concludes the case in favor of the mining company by announcing:

> For all the reasons given, my decision must be for the defendants. The claims of the plaintiffs for radical legal title to the territories in question are rejected. This title lies, as before, with the Crown. The claims of the Aborigines do not accord with the provisions

of English Common Law, which, though imported, is nonetheless, perhaps regrettably, the law of the land.

We see scenes of renewed blasting explorations and shots of tornadoes similar to those that opened the film. Watson, an Aboriginal ex-Air Force pilot, flies off, together with the second principal elder, Dayipu, in an old military propeller transport plane that has been given to the Aborigines by the mining company as partial compensation for the land rights, singing "My Baby Does the Hanky Panky" as he does so. An older woman, Mrs. Shrelow, in a kind of metaphorical echo of the patience of the Aborigines in sitting to resist the mining company's bulldozers, waits outside mining tunnels for her lost dog to turn up.

Throughout the negotiations and the trial between the mining company and the Aborigines, Hackett has grown increasingly disenchanted with the company and its plans. To Miliritbi he says, "I wish the world was as clear to me. I studied rocks and geological strata. I know that the earth is round and that it moves. But what shape the universe is and where it's going, I don't know." During a visit together to the mining company's urban headquarters, Hackett, Miliritbi, Dayipu, and Ferguson twice get stuck in an elevator—an image of the failure of progress. Between these two episodes, Hackett in a lunch restaurant says to the others "we're not really at this table at all. We're still stuck in that damned lift." Back in the mining camp, Hackett reports a nightmare to the dog lady. At the very end, Hackett turns on a radio that is broadcasting an Argentinian soccer match and then leaves the radio with an Aboriginal child. He visits the anthropologist Arnold, outside Arnold's corrugated tin hut, to ask, "are these easy to come by?" When Arnold tells him, "there's my old water tank still out there," Hackett walks off, carrying a bedroll and pack, away from Arnold and the camera, into a field of slag heaps, all but disappearing into the vast landscape.

Where the Green Ants Dream is both didactic and somewhat
episodic—there are further miniature subplots involving Aboriginal
children singing Christian hymns, Aboriginal elders sitting in a
grocery store to dream on the site of a dreaming tree that has been
cut down, a crazed scientist who describes how green ants are attuned
to magnetic fields, as well as Mrs. Shrelow and her dog. Vincent
Canby in his review remarks that Herzog "deals with this narrative
efficiently, but almost reluctantly, as if he couldn't care less about what
happens next."[27] More troublesome is the fact that the didactic theme
and the dramatic action are brought together in the figure of Hackett
in a way that is unconvincing, so that the message of the film seems
merely imposed on the material and argued rather than dramatically
achieved. Thomas Elsaesser observes that "Hackett is altogether too
resigned a participant to be suddenly seized by the 'wrath of God'
or the madness within, to be affected by anything stronger than self-
doubt and the general malaise of losing faith in Western civilization."[28]
In addition, Herzog's signature images of nature—the sweeping
tornadoes, the pans of vast landscapes of slag heaps and sand hills—
seem ill suited to close attention to genuine, specific legal and political
issues. As Elsaesser puts it:

> In an effort to close off one kind of transparency (that which
> classical narrative gives) [in favor of the ecstatic image], a
> structure of meaning imposes itself on Herzog's images that can
> only be called manichean: if the level on which the film is meant
> to work is cosmic, then the issue he chooses is too politically
> urgent, and the case too specific, for the metaphysical fiction to

---

[27]Vincent Canby, "Review of *Where the Green Ants Dream*," *New York Times*, February 8,
1985.

[28]Elsaesser, Thomas, "An Anthropologist's Eye: *Where the Green Ants Dream*," in *The Films
of Werner Herzog*, ed. Corrigan (1986), p. 138.

become convincing, especially with Hackett as a concession to conventional film dramaturgy acting as the story's (inadequate) central consciousness.[29]

Despite, however, its "slightly self-righteous tone," clumsy plot, and didacticism, *Where the Green Ants Dream* is intermittently visually stunning. It is difficult not to be moved by the signature Herzogian pans of vast, empty landscapes and the close-ups of the patient, dignified faces of the Aborigines as they sit in resistance, chant, or play the digeridoo. In the Foreword to his *Philosophical Remarks*, the philosopher Ludwig Wittgenstein wrote that:

> [The] spirit [of this book] is different from the one which informs the vast stream of European and American civilization in which all of us stand. *That* spirit expresses itself in an onwards movement, in building ever larger and more complicated structures; the other in striving after clarity and perspicuity in no matter what structure. The first tries to grasp the world by way of its periphery—in its variety; the second at its centre—in its essence. And so the first adds one construction to another, moving on and up, as it were, from one stage to the next, while the other remains where it is and what it tries to grasp is always the same.[30]

Both the Aborigines in their stoicism and Herzog in his filmic attentions to them and to landscape show something of Wittgenstein's spirit. Whatever the benefits of modern industrial-commercial life are—and they are considerable—in enabling increased human longevity, ease, control of a difficult

---

[29]Ibid., pp. 151–2.
[30]Ludwig Wittgenstein, *Philosophical Remarks*, ed. Rush Rhees, trans. Raymond Hargreaves and Roger White (Oxford: Basil Blackwell, 1975), p. 7.

environment, liberty, and individuality, one can also worry, along with Wittgenstein, the Aborigines, and Herzog, that modern life also includes too much undirected busyness, narcissism, and suppression of cultural marginality.

Thematically, *Gesualdo: Death for Five Voices* (1995) is Herzog's fullest meditation on the nature of history and the possibility and character of eruptions of meaning within it. The film is a selective, stylized biography of the Italian madrigal composer Carlo Gesualdo (1566–1613), including performances of his madrigals by two professional ensembles, the Italian *Il Complesso Barocco*, founded and directed by Alan Curtis, and the English *Gesualdo Consort of London*, directed by Gerald Place. Two central facts fundamentally shape Herzog's interest in Gesualdo. First, as a composer, Gesualdo was wildly out of step with and ahead of his time. As Herzog puts it, "while his other work is more within the context of his epoch, with the *Sixth Book of Madrigals* Gesualdo all of a sudden seemed to step four hundred years ahead of his time, composing music we hear only from Stravinsky onwards" (Cronin, 312–13). Second, early in his own career, it seemed to Herzog that Gesualdo spoke to him directly, across the gulf of the intervening history.

> When I left school I sensed a huge void so I dug into music with a ferocious intensity but no guidance from anyone. I started with Heinrich Schütz, and from there to Bach, Orlando di Lasso Carissimi, then Beethoven and the modern composers. Later I encountered Gesualdo's *Sixth Book of Madrigals*, a moment of absolute enlightenment for me. I was so excited I called up Florian Fricke at three in the morning. "Everyone who is into music knows about Gesualdo," he said after half an hour of my raving. "You sound as if you have discovered a new planet." But for me that's exactly what it felt like, as if I had found something tremendous within our

solar system, and out of that sprang a film about Gesualdo which I
carried within me for many years.[31]

Herzog's experience of Gesualdo thus amounts to what Benjamin
describes as an image, in this case an acoustic one, that "attain[s] to
legibility only at a particular time"[32] that is distinctly disjoint from
the time of the image's production, as it suddenly finds the audience
to which it speaks or flashes up. "Thus, to Robespierre ancient Rome
was a past charged with now-time, a past which he blasted out of
the continuum of history" in a "tiger's leap into the past."[33] That is,
the needs and capacities for reception of a subsequent present make
available the radically new reception of something that had been
otherwise dismissed or ignored. The communication of meaning is
significantly detached from intended audiences and the intervening
passage of time.

Every present day is determined by the images that are synchronic
with it: each "now" is the now of a particular recognizability. In
it, truth is charged to the bursting point with time. (This point of
explosion, and nothing else, is the death of the *intentio*, which thus
coincides with the birth of authentic historical time, the time of
truth. …) The image that is read—which is to say, the image in the
now of its recognizability—bears to the highest degree the imprint
of the perilous critical moment on which all reading is founded.[34]

---

[31] Herzog, *Herzog on Herzog* (New York: Farrar, Straus, and Giroux, 2002), p. 258; Cronin, p. 305 is identical, but lacks the final independent clause.

[32] Benjamin, *The Arcades Project*, N3,1, p. 462.

[33] Benjamin, "On the Concept of History," in Benjamin, *Selected Writings*, Vol. 4, Thesis 14, p. 395.

[34] Ibid., N3,1, pp. 462–3.

That Gesualdo spoke to Herzog—that his acoustic images achieved recognizability in Herzog's reception of them—is a function of their particular chromatic intensity that affords an interruptive shock effect something like the effects at which Herzog aims in his most striking signature landscape images. Jeffrey Kauffman speculates that "it might be generally accurate if perhaps slightly misleading to state that in a way [Gesualdo] was the Werner Herzog of the late Renaissance and nascent Baroque periods, an artist who consistently broke perceived 'rules' in his creative life while also being a bit hard to handle in his personal dealings."[35]

"A bit hard to handle in his personal dealings" is a significant understatement. As the movie details, Gesualdo murdered his first wife, Dona Maria d'Avalos, along with her lover, having caught them in flagrante delicto. After having servants shoot the couple and stab them with spears, Gesualdo returned to the bedroom in order to stab his wife with a knife another twenty-eight times in order to make sure that the job was done. Unproven but plausible enough rumor has it that he subsequently had their son killed, on the suspicion that the child was not in fact his, by leaving him in a cradle hung from an archway for three days, while a choir below sang his madrigals. Coupled with the historically transgressive character of his music, these facts about his personal life raise issues, for Herzog and for us, about possible affinities (if not always with such extreme elements) between madness, egoism, mania, and creativity. As Alex Ross notes:

> If Gesualdo had not committed such shocking acts, we might not pay such close attention to his music. But if he had not written such shocking music we would not care so much about his deeds.

---

[35]Jeffrey Kauffman, March 15, 2016 review of the Blu-Ray release of *Gesualdo: Death for Five Voices*, archived at http://www.blu-ray.com/movies/Gesualdo-Death-for-5-Voices-Blu-ray/148317/#Review.

Many bloodier crimes have been forgotten; it's the nexus of high art and foul play that catches our fancy. ... We wonder whether the violence of the art and the violence of the man emanated from the same demonic source.[36]

Erotic impulses toward the making of music, art, literature, film, and philosophy, among many other things, may bear family resemblances not only to one another but also to more directly sexual and violent impulses. This may be a thought that lies behind Herzog's remark that though "most of the stories in the film are completely invented and staged, yet they contain the most profound possible truths about Gesualdo. I think of all my 'documentaries', *Death for Five Voices* is the one that really runs amok, and it is one of the films closest to my heart."[37]

In fact, the account of both Gesualdo's music and the events of his life is fairly straightforward. Stories about the murders and other oddities of Gesualdo's life are presented by the two music directors, along with analyses of his music, illustrated by performances by the choirs. Further details about the life are provided by caretakers of Gesualdo's castle and house in Naples, as well as by local residents, all of whom are pleased to tell tales in order to promote tourism. There are also, however, a number of distinctly odd interjections. A bagpiper walks through and plays in the run-down Castle Gesualdo, telling us that he comes once a week in order to keep sealed up in the cracks of the walls the evil ghost of Gesualdo that must not leave the castle. Two cooks describe and recreate part of Gesualdo's 125-course wedding menu for 1000 guests that included 2000 oysters, 25 trays of

---

[36]Alex Ross, "Prince of Darkness: The Murders and Madrigals of Don Carlo Gesualdo," *The New Yorker* 87, 41 (December 19 and 26, 2011), pp. 84–92.

[37]Herzog, *Herzog on Herzog*, p. 260; compare the very similar Cronin, p. 312 that omits the final independent clause.

eels, 15 trays of quail, 120 young goats, and 25 loins of veal. A woman who claims to be the reincarnation of Maria d'Avalos runs through the castle. When the camera catches up with her, stopped, she sings parts of a Gesualdo madrigal, accompanied by the boom box she is carrying, and she reports that she lives in a small, red damask box near the column, high up by the chandelier, in the La Scala opera house in Milan. The director of an institute for the mentally ill reports that he has two patients who both believe they are Gesualdo, "and I absolutely cannot allow them to meet one another." A museum director reads a letter by Gesualdo to his alchemist, asking for help in deciphering obscure signs on a clay disk from the third or fourth century. The disk "remains a mystery to this day." Digressions from the plot of Gesualdo's life and the analysis and performance of his music though they are, what these interjections have in common is that each of them involves some kind of excessive reaction to or investment in Gesualdo, his life, and his music. They hyperbolize the thought that Gesualdo's life and music have flashed up across time to speak to them now, in ways that undermine and fracture more ordinary commitments and practices.

This same power to speak suddenly and disruptively across time is explicitly ascribed to Gesualdo's music. Alan Curtis, the conductor of *Il Complesso Barocco*, reads to us from Dr. Charles Burney's 1789 *A General History of Music*, according to which Gesualdo's music displays "the least regularity of design, phraseology, rhythm, or indeed anything remarkable in these madrigals, except unprincipled modulation and the perpetual embarrassments and inexperience of an amateur." Burney describes Gesualdo's masterpiece madrigal "Moro, lasso" ("I die, alas, in my suffering") in particular as containing "harsh, crude, and licentious modulation, not only repugnant to every rule of transition at present established but extremely shocking and disgusting to the ear." Yet 400 years after Gesualdo's life, Curtis tells us,

Stravinsky made a pilgrimage to Gesualdo's village in order to honor him. A complete performance of "Molto, lasso" ("I die, alas, in my suffering,/And the one who could give me life,/Alas, kills me and will not help me./O sorrowful fate,/the one who could give me life,/Alas, gives me death") follows. Twelve minutes later, following an interview with the current Prince d'Avalos and Gerald Place's account of the last sixteen years of Gesualdo's life, Alan Curtis tells us about his own early experiences of Gesualdo's music.

> When I first heard Gesualdo's music in college, forty years ago back in Michigan, I didn't find it beautiful. I found it fascinating, but difficult. And of course he was a very difficult man, and he wrote very difficult music. He also lived in a difficult time, but a time when people took risks, and there was adventure, excitement, as there still is in Italy. And there is still much risk-taking, and I think that's one of the clues to Gesualdo. Performers also must take risks, and be dangerous. And then the beauty of this wild music comes forth.

These lines are very close to Herzog's own thoughts about risk, adventure, the past, the present, and wild beauty.

The film then ends with shots of a pageant taking place in the town square of Gesualdo, featuring a boy-cherub fitted into a harness and flying along a wire across the square ("I'm an angel come from heaven"), riders jousting at a dummy, and close order drills with banners. After Curtis's speech we see medium shots of the pageant performers, until, as we hear a cell phone ringing, the camera closes in on a single footman in a medieval outfit. Answering the phone, he says "everything's fine here. Yeah, I saw it but not like that. It's not the same. There's a difference, right? Mum, listen, I already told you. I'll take the jockey and the horse home first. No, in half an hour. The Gesualdo film is finishing up"—an exchange that was staged by

Herzog (Cronin, 314). In close-up, the footman looks straight into the camera for thirteen seconds; the credits then roll over him for another ten seconds, until the scene fades to black as the credits continue.

The significance of this final sequence is that it is evidently itself an instance of risk-taking. There is no direct connection to the narrative of the film, other than the fact that the pageant takes place in the town square of Gesualdo; its parataxis relative to the narrative is an instance of unusual filmic modulation that echoes Gesualdo's unusual vocal modulations. The sequence is markedly and self-consciously both an artifice and a meditation on how, if at all, history might mean something to anyone now. As the footman looks directly and unwaveringly at us, we are challenged to think about why we are looking at him in his costume. Why is he there in the movie, costumed in this way? Why is this scene there? Who is speaking to us visually, how, and about what? The wager of the sequence, and one that Herzog makes often, is that it will flash up in its legibility to us now, given our current needs and possibilities, in a way that might motivate us

Figure 14 *The footman faces the camera: "the Gesualdo film is finishing up," from* Death for Five Voices *(1995).*

toward more animated life, if we are but alert enough both to our own circumstances and to what we see.

Why and how human beings first began to record the circumstances of their lives visually is the topic at the center of *Cave of Forgotten Dreams* (2010). Chauvet Cave was discovered in southern France, about 400 miles from Paris, in 1994. Sealed up in it by a rock slide 20,000 years ago that had covered any visible entrances are images on the cave walls of horses, bison, rhinos, lions, and other animals—images that were produced some 32,000 years ago, making them more than twice as old, we are told, as any other surviving images. Prompted by a *New Yorker* article about Chauvet, Herzog, and a three-man film crew (with Herzog doing the cold panel lights, powered by battery packs) were allowed into the cave for one to four hours per day during late March and early April 2010. While Herzog writes that "of all my films, *Cave of Forgotten Dreams* probably comes closest to the definition of a documentary as we are accustomed to using the word," he also observes that he "went in as a poet, hoping to activate the audience's imagination. If *Cave of Forgotten Dreams* were full only of scientific facts, it would be instantly forgettable" (Cronin, 410). As is typical for him, Herzog is as much interested in others' reactions to and understandings of the cave images—how they flash up for others—as he is in the images themselves. The roster of people whose work and thoughts he traces includes Jean Clottes (the former head of scientific research at Chauvet), the archaeologist (and former circus performer) Julien Monney, the paleontologist Michel Phillippe, the current Chauvet research manager Jean-Michel Geneste, the art historians Gilles Tosello and Carole Fritz, the archaeologists Dominique Baffier, Valérie Feruglio, Nicolas Conard, and Wulf Hein, and the master perfumer Maurice Marin. In each case, Herzog is interested not only in what they know, but also in how and what these images mean to them. As Manohla Dargis observes in her *New York Times* review, "much like [Julien Monney] and Ms. Deschamps, the explorer who cried out 'They were here' on seeing a painted mammoth, many of the researchers in the documentary seem deeply moved by the cave. In some ways they are communing with the dead, summoning up the eternally lost."[38] This is equally true of Herzog himself in filming the cave images.

Strikingly, the cave seems to have been used by human beings exclusively for artistic-ritual purposes. From the fact that it contains only animal bones, not human ones, "scientists have determined that humans never lived in the cave. They used it only for paintings and possibly ceremonies." The images they produced there "burst onto the scene like a sudden explosive event. It is as if the modern human soul had awakened here." What Herzog must mean by this is not that some component or part of the biological being suddenly burst into being or became on its own either conscious or effective, but rather that here and in similar contexts human beings suddenly began through ritual and representation to live and act as distinctly meaning-making and cultural beings. In response to Herzog's questions, "Do you think that the paintings in Chauvet Cave were somehow the beginning of the modern human soul? What constitutes humanness?," Jean-Michel Geneste replies:

> Humanness is a, is a, a very good adaptation with the, in the world. So, the … the human society needs to adaptate to the landscape, to the other beings, the animals, to other human groups. And to communicate something. To communicate it to—And to inscribe the memory on very, uh, specific and hard things, like walls, like pieces of wood, like, uh, like bones. This is, uh, invention of Cro-Magnon. … But with the invention of the figuration—figuration

---

[38]Manohla Dargis, "Herzog Finds His Inner Cave Man," *New York Times*, April 28, 2011.

of animals, of men, of things—it's a way of communication between humans and with a future, to evocate the past, to transmit information that is very better than language, than an overall communication. And this invention is still the same in our world today, with this camera, for example.

In *The Birth of Tragedy*, Nietzsche speculates that "the god himself made himself present to his celebrants" in the early Dionysian rites involving "extravagant sexual licentiousness … [where] the most horrible savage instincts were released."[39] With time and repetition, however, this ritual was replaced by something self-consciously manufactured and staged, where Dionysius is imitatively portrayed rather than being literally re-present, and it is at this point that human beings become explicitly aware of themselves as self-conscious agents and agents of culture, able both to generate and to respond to representations. Ritual and repetition are central to the emergence of self-consciousness and awareness of being governed by norms. It is in this sense that the ritual production and use of images at Chauvet has a claim to be regarded as a site of the earliest exercises of powers of human ensoulment. "Homo spiritualis"—those who adopt points of view outside their own person and who traffic in ritual and representation—"would be better than homo sapiens" as a name for human beings, Julien Monney tells us.

It is true, as Monney remarks, that "life must have been very different for these people from the way we live now," and one must in order to understand these people compare the Chauvet images to examples of rock art from other cultures. "You must start from the cave and then go outside." Nonetheless, the images they produced

---

[39]Friedrich Nietzsche, *The Birth of Tragedy*, trans. Walter Kaufmann (New York: Random House, 1967), §2, p. 39.

are neither primitive nor unaccomplished. "The painters of the cave seem to speak to us from a familiar yet distant universe," including using contemporary motifs such as bull plus woman and involving careful attention to the cave wall contours, point of view, and shading. "They've played with the contrast and shape of the wall" in order to produce dramatic effects and an illusion of movement, Carole Fritz tells us. "These aren't primitive scribblings on the cave walls, like the first attempts of young children. Art emerged fully accomplished, tens of thousands of years ago; Greek, Roman, Renaissance and modern art never got any better. This is the true origin of art, even of the modern human soul, and there is something wonderfully confident about it" (Cronin, 408–9).

Something connects us with the image-makers of the Chauvet caves, in being makers of meaning and traffickers in representations and points of view. "We can go back with our imagination" in order to appreciate the images and their uses, the master perfumer Maurice Maurin tells us, to which Herzog adds, "With [Maurin's] sense of wonder, the cave transforms into an enchanted world of the imaginary where time and space lose their meaning." The archaeologist Wulf Hein, dressed in reindeer fur and leather, demonstrates the pentatonic scale on a Paleolithic flute "made out of the radius of a vulture" and then plays "The Star Spangled Banner" on it. Commenting on the dramatic rock bridge, the Pont d'Arc, that sits in a striking landscape near the cave, Herzog asks, "Could this be our connection to them? This staging of the landscape as an operatic event does not belong to the romanticists alone. Stone Age man might have had a similar sense of inner landscapes, and it seems natural that there's a whole cluster of Paleolithic caves right around here." Understanding human meaning-making requires the exercise of imagination in order to adopt new points of view and to appreciate from the inside what human beings were doing with the objects and images they made, where the makings and doings in question are always inherently social, expressive, communicative, and spiritual.

Cave of Forgotten Dreams ends with an odd postscript showing mutant albino crocodiles swimming in heated runoff water from a nuclear power plant along the Rhone, about twenty miles from Chauvet. (In fact—it is unclear whether Herzog knew this at the time of the shooting—they are naturally occurring, non-mutant alligators, imported from Louisiana.) The credits begin to roll over an extreme close-up head of a crocodile (alligator), looking straight into the camera and at us. Just before this there is an oddly compelling shot of two alligators, shown in profile, mirroring each other, as their snouts stick just above the surface of the water and almost touch.

It is initially unclear exactly why these images are there. They serve no direct expository function. Herzog must, however, have wanted to stress both the artifactuality of images—that they are made by human beings—and the fact that they can on their own evoke interest, wonder, awe, and mystery, without having any

Figure 15 *The white "crocodiles" mirror each other, from* Cave of Forgotten Dreams *(2010).*

directly linguistic message. And Herzog reminds us of our own temporality and finitude, in asking about the crocodiles, "Looking at the paintings, what will they make of them?" To stress these things is to stress connections between the Chauvet cave image-makers (and those who used them) and Herzog himself as a filmmaker (and his audiences who view his films).

The most striking and memorable sequence in *Cave* occurs about one third of the way in (25:06–26:00). In response to Herzog's question "Could it be how they set up fires in Chauvet Cave, there's evidence that they cast their own shadows against the panels of horses, for example?," Jean-Michel Geneste replies, "The fires were necessary to look at the paintings and maybe towards staging people around. When you look with the flame, with moving light, you can imagine people dancing with the shadows." This reply is then followed by twenty-nine seconds of Fred Astaire's famous Shadow Dance from *Swing Time* (1936), as Geneste continues to explain that "black shadows on white walls were the first representations." This sequence is an utterly compelling presentation of both our similarities to and differences from Paleolithic image makers, as we each use representations to try to transcend our own individual viewpoints and to come to terms with our lives in situ within nature that we, unlike other animals, know are finite.

The tension and interplay between cultural affordances as sources of meaning and markedly individual reactions to those affordances are at the heart of *Encounters at the End of the World* (2007). That cultures—many of them, in different ways—are crucial for orientation, self-consciousness, and an ability to make sense of things is made clear by William Jirsa, a computer expert and Ho-chunk (Winnebago, a member of the Sioux family) linguist, who has been forced to abandon his Ph.D. research and has washed up in Antarctica, where he now runs a greenhouse at McMurdo Station.

So, just imagine, you know, 90% of languages will be extinct, probably in my lifetime. It's a catastrophic impact to an ecosystem to talk about that kind of extinction. Culturally, we're talking about the same thing. I mean, you know, what if, what if you lost all of Russian literature or something like that or Russian, you know, if you took all of the Slavic languages and just, they went away, you know, and no more Tolstoy.

In reply, Herzog is quick to agree with him.

It occurred to me that in the time we spent with him in the greenhouse, possibly three or four languages had died. In our efforts to preserve endangered species, we seem to overlook something equally important. To me, it is a sign of a deeply disturbed civilization where tree huggers and whale huggers in their weirdness are acceptable while no one embraces the last speakers of a language.

Yet it is equally important that cultures and languages do not simply produce, embody, and transmit meaning smoothly and independently of the distinct reactions of the people who grow up within them or otherwise encounter them. In any given culture, alienation is possible, and McMurdo Station and the other research facilities on Antarctica are filled with individuals who have left their home cultures—sometimes fleeing political oppression, sometimes just looking for new and different forms of sense—in order to move to the "end of the world." As Jirsa puts it:

I like to say, if you take everybody who's not tied down they all sort of fall down to the bottom of the planet, so that's how we got here, you know. We're all at loose ends, and here we are together. I remember when I first got down here I sort of enjoyed the sensation of recognizing people with my travel markings. I was like hey, these are my people—PhDs washing dishes and linguists on a continent with no languages.

We all as individuals bear our own "travel markings," and in order to feel that our lives are actively our own, we need not only a grammar or framework provided by a culture, but also the sense of effectively expressing one's individuality in one's activities, to some extent against the grain of an anonymizing general culture, though also along with a few odd, like-minded individuals.

The individuals in the film who are the primary subjects of Herzog's encounters all markedly display the fact that they have left the places of their upbringing and prior experiences in an effort to find something different in Antarctica. Herzog frequently begins his conversations with them by asking, "And how does it happen that we are encountering each other here at the end of the world?," and their answers recount their itineraries. There is Scott Rowland, who drives "Ivan, the Terra Bus," the largest vehicle on the continent, but who has previously been a banker in Colorado and a Peace Corps worker in Guatemala, where he had had to learn the Mayan dialect Keck`Chi and where he was prosecuted for and acquitted of child-stealing. Stefan Pashov, "Philosopher, Forklift Driver," was born in Sofia, Bulgaria and has traveled to eighty-five different countries. The glaciologist Douglas MacAyeal "can feel the rumble of the glaciers" in his dreams as he tries to understand the enormous glacier B-15 "as a living being that's dynamic, that's producing change." Ryan A. Evans, "Filmmaker, Cook" runs and explains the operations of the Frosty Boy dessert machine in the McMurdo Station cafeteria. David Pacheco, a journeyman plumber, tells us he is part Apache and descended from the Aztec and Inca royal families, as indicated by the fact that lower joint creases opposite his knuckles on the inside of his fingers line up in a perfectly straight line. Sam Bowser, a cell biologist and the head of the scientific field team, investigates underwater tree foraminifera, and he finds in them "borderline intelligence, yeah, at the single cell level. I mean, it's a manifestation of the best of our abilities, really, the way that they build their shells. It's almost art." In between lab work and dives to collect the creatures, he likes to show 1950s science fiction films to his team, and he practices for and plays a celebratory rock concert at midnight on the roof of a small shelter. The computer expert Karen Joyce drove a garbage truck across Africa, where she was kidnapped by the military in Uganda, was stuck in the desert with minimal water for five days, suffered from malaria, and was chased through swamps by angry elephants. She hitchhiked from Ecuador to Peru, riding inside one of three giant sewer pipes on the back of a flatbed truck. At a "Freak Event" entertainment night, she demonstrates how to "travel as hand luggage" by climbing into and having herself zipped up inside a carry-on duffel bag. Libor Zicha, a utility mechanic who has escaped "from behind the Iron Curtain," keeps a backpack packed at all times, including not only a sleeping bag and cooking utensils, but also a folding kayak paddle and an inflatable boat.

In one way or another—and necessarily so for Antarctica, which has no indigenous peoples—these figures are all itinerants and seekers. Stefan Pashov captures this point in remarking that:

I think that it's a logical place to find each other, because this place works almost as a natural selection for people that have this intention to jump off the margin of the map, and we all meet here, where all the lines of the map converge. There is no point that is south of the South Pole. And I think there is a fair amount of the population here which are full-time travelers and part-time workers. So, yes, those are the professional dreamers. They dream all the time, and I think, through them, the great cosmic dreams come into fruition, because the universe dreams through our dreams, and I think that there is many different ways for the reality to bring itself forward, and dreaming is definitely one of those ways.

Pashov's remarks are followed by Herzogian signature shots of vast ice fields with mountains in the background and labyrinthine ice caves with intricate icicle formations, stalactites, and stalagmites, backed by somewhat ethereal and vaguely Celtic music for violin, cello, and organ. As the sequence concludes, Herzog comments in voice-over that "as banal as McMurdo appears, it turns out that it is filled with these professional dreamers," as he turns to introducing us to further members of his cast of itinerants.

It is a serious question how anyone can achieve and sustain a sense of meaningful orientation within relationships and circuits of activity, set within the larger frameworks of nature and history: how anyone might effectively pursue one's dreams. In *The Theory of the Novel*, Georg Lukács characterizes human beings within modern industrial-commercial life as suffering from "transcendental homelessness."[40] In no longer living within "a rounded world of presence of meaning"[41]—often a coercive and repetitive one—human beings no longer have open to them the kind of heroism that incarnates in an exemplary way the values shared throughout all known culture. What remains for human beings to do, in life or in art, is always tinged with contingency, irony, interiority (a sense of human powers not fitly and fully expressed), and absurdity. In *Encounters at the End of the World*, Herzog describes the opening of the Antarctic—

---

[40]Georg Lukács, *The Theory of the Novel*, trans. Anna Bostock (Cambridge, MA: MIT Press, 1971), p. 41.
[41]Ibid., p. 33.

the last unexplored region of the earth—by Shackleton, Amundsen, and Scott. Shackelton in particular, he tell us, undertook his voyages "for personal fame and the glory of the British Empire." Echoing Lukács, Herzog then adds that:

> The Empire started to fade into the abyss of history. … [Shackleton's still-preserved original hut, with its shelves of hundred-year old cans] looks now like an extinct supermarket. On a cultural level it meant the end of adventure. … Human adventure in its original sense lost its meaning, became an issue for the *Guinness Book of World Records*. … From there on [adventure] degenerated into absurd quests. A Frenchman crossed the Sahara desert in his car set in reverse gear, and I am waiting for the first barefoot runner on the summit of Everest, or the first one hopping into the South Pole on a pogo stick.

He then introduces us to Ashrita Furman, Multiple World Record Holder, who "had this idea of breaking a Guinness record in every continent," showing him somersaulting, running with a full milk bottle on his head—he holds world records in both—and hopping on a pogo stick. The obvious issue is what, if any, sorts of fully meaningful activity and achievement are possible for us now, we moderns, in contrast with such absurdities.

For Herzog, no answer will come from experts grasping a Platonic *logos*, the will of God, or the plot of Providence. Nor will it come from the physical natural sciences, where the very idea of self-consciously undertaken and recognized adventure has no place.[42] Human beings will

---

[42]Compare the philosopher Georg Bertram: "The human form of life is one that is reflexively constituted in a particular way. Human beings are not what they are by nature alone. Nor are they constituted as what they are as a simple result of tradition. Rather, human beings must also always determine what they are ever anew. The human being is what he is always also through the fact that he takes a stance." Bertram, *Kunst als menschliche Praxis: Eine Äesthetik* (Berlin: Suhrkamp, 2014), pp. 12–13; my translation.

remain what Hegel calls amphibious animals, torn between the demands and possibilities of spirit and meaningful life, on the one hand, and the standing fact of immersion within senseless nature on the other. At best, we might become, with Herzog, halted travelers, struck by some sudden sense of either dramatic achievement and promise or dramatic failure in particular places and on the parts of particular individuals within courses of embodied activity. We might, as the philosopher David Wiggins once put it, hope to find glimmers of temporarily meaningful activities amid standing circumstances of defeat, as we try to "think in both directions, down from point to the human activities which answer to it, and up from activities … to forms of life in which [human beings] by their nature can find point."[43] "Self-presence and self-mastery are," as Georg Bertram puts it, "not self-evidently given, but rather much more a vanishing point within human practices."[44]

It will require a particular courage and resoluteness to seek out and respond to such achievements and defeats of selfhood, and to do so without fantasy, sentimentality, narcissistic projection, or, in the end, despair. In the risks it takes, and in its ranges of frequent spectacular artistic success as well as sometime failure, Herzog's work displays in full measure this kind of courage and resoluteness. Paul Cronin describes Herzog as "showing us how to transcend the bankrupt world into which we are sinking, one choked with anti-intellectualism, cynicism, consumerism, fear, cowardice, vulgarity, extremism, laziness and narcissism,"[45] as he works, in Bertram's terms, "against a threatening petrification"[46] of the human.

---

[43]David Wiggins, "Truth, Invention, and the Meaning of Life." *Proceedings of the British Academy* 62 (1976), pp. 331–78, at pp. 374–5.

[44]Bertram, *Kunst als menschliche Praxis*, p. 14; my translation.

[45]Cronin, "Visionary Vehemence," p. xxxix.

[46]Bertram, *Kunst als menschliche Praxis*, p. 66; my translation.

There are risks to this work. Some will find some of Herzog's films sentimental or narcissistic. Some will find his emphasis on individual heroism in extreme circumstances (of either defeat or exemplary bodily performance) too insensitive to genuine possibilities of adventure and meaning in more ordinary life, including the spheres of family life, occupation, and political citizenship. Herzog notes himself that late in his career, prompted in part by his encounter with Delbert Burkett and Delbert's account of his failures as a father in *Into the Abyss* (2011) and partly "as the father of three grown children out in the world living their own lives," he has come in relation to family life to "see things with fresh eyes" (Cronin, 425). "Family loyalty is a priceless gift" (Cronin, 425). Even here, however, finding meaning and value is not a matter of simple, automatic givens; "it's more about insight and actively dwelling on such things" (Cronin, 425), as we must make and re-make our lives—familial, occupational, religious, athletic, musical, performative, and otherwise—by developing and exercising qualities of character and attention. In presenting us throughout his films with what he calls in the director's commentary to *Encounters at the End of the World* "individuals who fell in love with the world," in circumstances of both achievement and defeat (including self-defeat), Herzog provides us with "short flickering moments of illumination, some kind of understanding of who we are" (Cronin, 414) that include some of the highest achievements of art in its sensuous presentation of who we are and might be.

Bibliography

Allen, Nick (2017), "Review of *Salt and Fire*," archived at: https://www.rogerebert.com/reviews/salt-and-fire-2017

Ames, Eric (2012), *Ferocious Reality: Documentary According to Werner Herzog*, Minneapolis, MN: University of Minnesota Press.

Aristotle (1941), *Physics*, trans. R. P. Hardie and R. K. Gaye, in Aristotle, *The Basic Works of Aristotle*, ed. Richard McKeon, New York: Random House.

Bazin, Andre (1967), "The Ontology of the Photographic Image" [1945], in *What Is Cinema?* trans. Hugh Gray, Berkeley, CA: University of California Press, pp. 9–16.

Benelli, Dana (1986), "The Cosmos and Its Discontents," in *The Films of Werner Herzog*, ed. Timothy Corrigan, London: Routledge, 1986, pp. 89–103.

Benjamin, Walter (1996), "The Life of Students," in Benjamin, *Selected Writings*, Vol. 1, 1913–26, eds Marcus Bullock and Michael W. Jennings, Cambridge, MA: Harvard University Press, pp. 37–48.

Benjamin, Walter (1999), *The Arcades Project*, trans. Howard Eiland and Kevin McLaughlin, Cambridge, MA: Harvard University Press.

Benjamin, Walter (2003), "On the Concept of History," trans. Harry Zohn, in Benjamin, *Selected Writings*, Vol. IV, 1938–1940, eds Howard Eiland and Michael W. Jennings, Cambridge, MA: Harvard University Press, pp. 389–400.

Bertram, Georg (2014), *Kunst als menschliche Praxis: Eine Äesthetik*, Berlin: Suhrkamp.

Blank, Les and James Bogan, eds (1984), *Burden of Dreams: Screenplay, Journals, Reviews, Photographs*. Berkeley, CA: North Atlantic Books.

Canby, Vincent (1971), "Sounding the Alarm on the Sahara," *New York Times*, October 8, 1971.

Canby, Vincent (1977), "Herzog's Pilgrims Hit the Road," *New York Times*, July 13, 1977.

Canby, Vincent (1985), 'Review of *Where the Green Ants Dream*," *New York Times*, February 8, 1985.

Carroll, Noël (1998), "Herzog, Presence, and Paradox," in *Interpreting the Moving Image*, ed. Carroll, Cambridge: Cambridge University Press, pp. 284–99.

Carter, Erica (2012), "Werner Herzog's African Sublime," in *A Companion to Werner Herzog*, ed. Brad Prager, Oxford: Wiley-Blackwell, pp. 329–355.

Cavell, Stanley (1979), *The World Viewed*, Enlarged Edition, Cambridge, MA: Harvard University Press.

Cavell, Stanley (1981), *The Senses of Walden: An Expanded Edition*, San Francisco, CA: North Point Press.

Cohen, Ted (2008), *Thinking of Others: On the Talent for Metaphor*, Princeton, NJ: Princeton University Press.

Cook, Roger F. (2012), "The Ironic Ecstasy of Werner Herzog: Embodied Vision in *The Great Ecstasy of Woodcarver Steiner*," in *A Companion to Werner Herzog*, ed. Brad Prager, pp. 281–300.

Corrigan, Timothy (1986), *The Films of Werner Herzog: Between Mirage and History*, ed. Timothy Corrigan, London: Routledge.

Cronin, Paul (2002), *Herzog on Herzog*, London: Faber and Faber.

Cronin, Paul (2014a), *Werner Herzog—A Guide for the Perplexed: Conversations with Paul Cronin*, London: Faber and Faber.

Cronin, Paul (2014b), "Visionary Vehemence: Ten Thoughts about Werner Herzog," in *Werner Herzog—A Guide for the Perplexed*, pp. xi–xli.

Csicsery, George Paul (1986), "*Ballad of the Little Soldier*: Werner Herzog in a Political Hall of Mirrors," *Film Quarterly* 39, 2 (Winter 1985–86), pp. 7–15.

Dargis, Manohla (2011), "Herzog Finds His Inner Cave Man," *New York Times*, April 28, 2011.

Davidson, Donald (1989), "Mental Events," in *Essays on Action and Events*, ed. Davidson, Oxford: Oxford University Press, pp. 207–24.

Del Caro, Adrian (2004), *Grounding the Nietzsche Rhetoric of Earth*, Berlin: de Gruyter.

Deleuze, Gilles (1978), "Nomad Thought," trans. Jacqueline Wallace, in *Semiotexte* III, 1, [*Nietzsche's Return*], pp. 12–21.

Descartes, René (1994), *The Principles of Philosophy*, in Descartes, *Discourse on Method, Meditations, and Principles*, trans. John Veitch, London: J. M. Dent.

Ebert, Roger (2017), *Herzog by Ebert*, Chicago, IL: University of Chicago Press.

Eldridge, Richard (2001), *The Persistence of Romanticism*, Cambridge: Cambridge University Press.

Eldridge, Richard (2008), *Literature, Life, and Modernity*, New York: Columbia University Press.

Eldridge, Richard (2014a), "Hegel's Account of the Unconscious and Why It Matters," *The Review of Metaphysics*, LXVII, 3, pp. 491–516.

Eldridge, Richard (2014b), "How Movies Think: Cavell on Film as a Medium of Art," *Estetika: The Central European Journal of Aesthetics* LI/VII, 1, pp. 3–20.

Eldridge, Richard (2016), *Images of History: Kant, Benjamin, Freedom, and the Human Subject*, Oxford: Oxford University Press.

Elsaesser, Thomas (1986), "An Anthropologist's Eye: *Where the Green Ants Dream*," in *The Films of Werner Herzog*, ed. Timothy Corrigan, London: Routledge, pp. 133–56.

Elster, Jon (1986), *An Introduction to Karl Marx*, Cambridge: Cambridge University Press.

Farrell, Frank B. (2004), *Why Does Literature Matter?* Ithaca, NY: Cornell University Press.

Freeman, Samuel (1994), "Political Liberalism and the Possibility of a Just Constitution," *Chicago-Kent Law Review* 69, 3, *Symposium on John Rawls Political Liberalism*, pp. 619–68.

Freud, Sigmund (2010), *Civilization and Its Discontents*, trans. James Strachey, New York: W. W. Norton & Company.

Frye, Northrop (1963), "The Drunken Boat," in *Romanticism Reconsidered*, ed. Northrop Frye, New York: Columbia University Press, pp. 1–15.

Golder, Herbert (2014), "Shooting on the Lam," in *Werner Herzog—A Guide for the Perplexed*, ed. Cronin, pp. 478–88.

Gorsozlu, Fuat (2014), "Political Liberalism and the Fate of Unreasonable People," *Touro Law Review* 30, 1, pp. 35–56.

Hacker, P. M. S. (2007), *Human Nature: The Categorial Framework*, Oxford: Blackwell.

Hadot, Pierre (1995), *Philosophy as a Way of Life: Spiritual Exercises from Socrates to Foucault*, trans. Michael Chase, Malden, MA: Wiley-Blackwell.

Halle, Randall (2012), "Perceiving the Other in *Land of Silence and Darkness*," in *A Companion to Werner Herzog*, ed. Brad Prager, pp. 487–509.

Hanssen, Beatrice (2002), "'Dichtermut' and 'Blödigkeit': Two Poems by Friedrich Hölderlin Interpreted by Walter Benjamin," in *Walter Benjamin and Romanticism*, eds, Beatrice Hanssen and Andrew Benjamin, New York: Continuum, pp. 139–62.

Harris, Stefanie (2012), "Moving Stills: Herzog and Photography," in *A Companion to Werner Herzog*, ed. Brad Prager, pp. 127–48.

Hegel, G. W. F. (1971), *Philosophy of Mind*, Part Three of the *Encyclopedia of Philosophical Sciences*, trans. William Wallace and A. V. Miller, Oxford: Clarendon Press.

Hegel, G. W. F. (1977), *Phenomenology of Spirit*, trans. A. V. Miller, Oxford: Clarendon Press.

Hegel, G. W. F. (1991), *Elements of the Philosophy of Right*, trans. H. B. Nisbet, ed. Allen W. Wood, Cambridge: Cambridge University Press.

Heidegger, Martin (1962), *Being and Time* [1927], trans. John Macquarrie and Edward Robinson, Oxford: Basil Blackwell.

Heidegger, Martin (1971), "The Origin of the Work of Art," trans. Albert Hofstadter, in Heidegger, *Poetry, Language, Thought*, New York: Harper & Row, pp. 15–88.

Heilman, Jeremy (2002), "Review of *Heart of Glass*, May 2, 2002, moviemartyr. com, archived at http://www.moviemartyr.com/1976/heartofglass.htm.

Herzog, Lena (2004), *Pilgrims: Becoming the Path Itself*, London: Periplus.

Herzog, Werner (1964), "Rebellen in Amerika: Zu Filmen des New American Cinema," in *Filmstudio*, pp. 55–60.

Herzog, Werner (1979), "Images at the Horizon," in *Herzog by Ebert*, ed. Roger Ebert, pp. 3–48.

Herzog, Werner (2004a), "Introduction," in *Pilgrims: Becoming the Path Itself*, ed. Lena Herzog, London: Periplus.

Herzog, Werner (2004b), "Werner Herzog, 2004," interview with Doug Aiken, *Index Magazine*, archived at http://www.indexmagazine.com/interviews/ werner_herzog.shtml.

Herzog, Werner (2010), "On the Absolute, the Sublime, and Ecstatic Truth," trans. Moira Weigel, *Arion* 17, 3, pp. 1–12.

Herzog, Werner (2015), *Of Walking in Ice*, trans. Martje Herzog and Alan Greenberg Minneapolis, MN: University of Minnesota Press.

Herzog, Werner (2017), *Scenarios*, trans. Martje Herzog and Alan Greenberg, Minneapolis, MN: University of Minnesota Press.

Hillman, Roger (2012), "Coming to Our Senses: The Viewer and Herzog's Sonic Worlds," in *A Companion to Werner Herzog*, ed. Brad Prager, pp. 168–86.

Hoberman, J. (1975), "Obscure Objects of Desire," *Village Voice*, February 19, 1975.

Homer (1990), *The Iliad*, trans. Robert Fagles, London: Penguin.

Horak, Jan-Christopher, "W. H., or the Mysteries of Walking in Ice," in *The Films of Werner Herzog*, ed. Timothy Corrigan, pp. 25–49.

Hüser, Rembert (2012), "Herzog's Chickenshit," in *A Companion to Werner Herzog*, ed. Brad Prager, pp. 445–65.

Jansen, Peter W., "innen/außen/innen: Funktionen von Raum und Landschaft [bei Herzog, Kluge, Straub]," in *Herzog/Kluge/Straub*, eds. Peter W. Jansen and Wolfram Schütte, München: Hanser.

Johnson, Laurie (2012), "Werner Herzog's Romantic Spaces," in *A Companion to Werner Herzog*, ed. Brad Prager, pp. 510–27.

Johnson, Laurie Ruth (2016), *Forgotten Dreams: Revisiting Romanticism in the Cinema of Werner Herzog*, Rochester, NY: Camden House.

Kant, Immanuel (2000), *The Critique of the Power of Judgment*, trans. Paul Guyer and Eric Matthews, Cambridge: Cambridge University Press.

Kauffman, Jeffrey, March 15, 2016 review of the Blu-Ray release of *Gesualdo: Death for Five Voices*, archived at http://www.blu-ray.com/movies/Gesualdo-Death-for-5-Voices-Blu-ray/148317/#Review.

Koch, Gertrud (1986), "Blindness as Insight: *Land of Silence and Darkness*," in *The Films of Werner Herzog*: ed. Timothy Corrigan, pp. 73–86.

Koepnick, Lutz (2012), "Archetypes of Emotion· Werner Herzog and Opera," in *A Companion to Werner Herzog*, ed. Brad Prager, pp. 149–67.

Koepnick, Lutz (2013), "Herzog's Cave: On Cinema's Unclaimed Past and Forgotten Futures," *Germanic Review: Literature, Culture, Theory* 88, 3, pp. 271–85.

Kolker, Robert Philip (1983), *The Altering Eye: Contemporary International Cinema*, Cambridge, England: Open Book Publishers.

Ladino, Jennifer K. (2009), "For the Love of Nature. Documenting Life, Death, and Animality in *Grizzly Man* and *March of the Penguins*," *ISLE: Interdisciplinary Studies in Literature and Environment* 16, 1, pp. 53–90.

Lear, Jonathan (2003), *Therapeutic Action: An Earnest Plea for Irony*, New York: Other Press.

Lear, Jonathan (2015), *A Case for Irony*, Cambridge, MA: Harvard University Press.

Lehman, Will (2012), "A March Into Nothingness: The Changing Course of Herzog's Indian Images," in *A Companion to Werner Herzog*, ed. Brad Prager, pp. 371–92.

Locke, John (1959), *An Essay Concerning Human Understanding*, New York: Dover.

Lukács, Georg (1971), *The Theory of the Novel*, trans. Anna Bostock, Cambridge, MA: MIT Press.

Marcuse, Herbert (1978), *The Aesthetic Dimension*, trans. and revised Herbert Marcuse and Erica Sherover, Boston: Beacon Press.

Merleau-Ponty, Maurice (2012), *Phenomenology of Perception*, trans. Donald A. Landes, New York: Routledge.

Nehamas, Alexander (1987), *Nietzsche: Life as Literature*, Cambridge, MA: Harvard University Press.

Nicodemus, Katja (2010), "Herr der Schmerzen," [Interview with Herzog], *Die Zeit* February 4, 2010, *Feuilleton*.

Nietzsche, Friedrich (1967), *The Birth of Tragedy*, trans. Walter Kaufmann, New York: Random House.

Nietzsche Friedrich (1974), *Werke: Kritische Gesamtausgabe*, eds Giorgio Colli and Mazzino Montinari, Vol. VII, Part 2, *Nachgelassene Fragmente*, Berlin: de Gruyter.

Nietzsche, Friedrich (1979), "On Truth and Lies in a Nonmoral Sense" [1873], in *Philosophy and Truth: Selections from the Nietzsche's Early Notebooks of the Early 1970's*, ed. and trans. Daniel Breazeale, Atlantic Highlands, NJ: Humanities Press.

Nietzsche, Friedrich (2002), *Beyond Good and Evil: Prelude to a Philosophy of the Future*, ed. Rolf-Peter Horstmann and Judith Norman, trans. Judith Norman, Cambridge: Cambridge University Press.

Nietzsche, Friedrich (2003), *Writings from the Late Notebooks*, ed. Rudiger Bittner, trans. Kate Sturge, Cambridge: Cambridge University Press.

Nietzsche, Friedrich (2006), *On the Genealogy of Morals*, ed. Keith Ansell-Pearson, trans. Carol Diethe, 2nd ed., Cambridge: Cambridge University Press.

Peucker, Brigitte (1986), "Literature and Writing in the Films of Werner Herzog," in *The Films of Werner Herzog*, ed. Timothy Corrigan, pp. 105–17.

Peucker, Brigitte (2012), "Herzog and Auteurism," in *A Companion to Werner Herzog*, ed. Brad Prager, pp. 35–57.

Prager, Brad (2007), *The Cinema of Werner Herzog: Aesthetic Ecstasy and Truth*, London: Wallflower Press.

Prager, Brad (2012), *A Companion to Werner Herzog*, ed. Brad Prager, Walden, MA: Wiley-Blackwell.

Rawls, John (1999), *A Theory of Justice*, rev. ed., Cambridge, MA: Harvard University Press.

Rentschler, Eric (1986), "The Politics of Vision: Herzog's *Heart of Glass*," in *The Films of Werner Herzog*, ed. Timothy Corrigan, pp. 159–81.

Rosen, Philip (2001), *Change Mummified: Cinema, Historicity, Theory*, Minneapolis, MN: University of Minnesota Press.

Ross, Alex (2011), "Prince of Darkness: The Murders and Madrigals of Don Carlo Gesualdo," *The New Yorker* 87, 41, December 19 and 26, 2011, pp. 84–92.

Ross, Alison (2015), *Walter Benjamin's Concept of the Image*, London: Routledge.

Ruf, Wolfgang (1972), "Land des Schweigens und der Dunkelheit," *Deutsche Kinemathek*, Sig. 55146.

Rush, Fred (2016), *Irony and Idealism: Rereading Schlegel, Hegel, and Kierkegaard*, Oxford: Oxford University Press.

Shapiro, Gary (1989), "How One Becomes What One Is Not," in *Nietzschean Narratives*, Bloomington, IN: Indiana University Press, pp. 142–67.

Singer, Alan (1986), "Comprehending Appearances: Werner Herzog's Ironic Sublime," in *The Films of Werner Herzog*, ed. Timothy Corrigan, pp. 183–205.

Steingröver, Reinhold (2012), "Encountering Werner Herzog at the End of the World," in *A Companion to Werner Herzog*, ed. Brad Prager, pp. 466–84.

Taylor, Charles (1993), *Sources of the Self*, Cambridge, MA: Harvard University Press.

Taylor, Diana (2007), "Remapping Genre through Performance: From 'American' to 'Hemispheric' Studies," *Publications of the Modern Language Association* 122, 5, pp. 1416–30.

Van Wert, William (1986), "Last Words: Observations on a New Language," in *The Films of Werner Herzog*, ed. Timothy Corrigan, pp. 51–71.

Wiggins, David (1976), "Truth, Invention, and the Meaning of Lite," *Proceedings of the British Academy* 62, pp. 331–78.

Wittgenstein, Ludwig (1975), *Philosophical Remarks*, ed. Rush Rhees, trans. Raymond Hargreaves and Roger White, Oxford: Basil Blackwell.

Wollheim, Richard (1980), *Painting as an Art*, Princeton, NJ: Princeton University Press.

Wordsworth, William (1965a) Lines Composed a Few Miles above Tintern Abbey," in Wordsworth, *Selected Poems and Prefaces*, ed. Jack Stillinger, Boston: Houghton Mifflin, pp. 108–11.

Wordsworth, William (1965b), "Preface to the Second Edition of *Lyrical Ballads* [1800]," in Wordsworth, *Selected Poems and Prefaces*, ed. Jack Stillinger, pp. 445–64.

Wordsworth, William (1965c), *The Prelude* [1850], in Wordsworth, *Selected Poems and Prefaces*, ed. Jack Stillinger, pp. 193–366.

Wordsworth, William (1965d), *Selected Poems and Prefaces*, ed. Jack Stillinger. Boston: Houghton-Mifflin.

Yacavone, Daniel (2015), *Film Worlds*, New York: Columbia University Press.

Index